Identifying American Furniture

Identifying American Furniture

A Pictorial Guide to Styles and Terms
Colonial to Contemporary

Second Edition, Revised and Expanded

Milo M. Naeve

W. W. Norton & Company
New York   London

W. W. Norton & Company, Inc.
500 Fifth Avenue
New York, New York 10110

W. W. Norton & Company, Ltd.
37 Great Russell Street
London WC1B 3NU

First published as a Norton paperback 1989.

First Edition published 1981.
First Edition, second printing 1982.
Second Edition, revised and expanded 1989.

The original publication of this book was made possible in part by funds from the sale of the Bicentennial State Histories, which were supported by the National Endowment for the Humanities.

Library of Congress Cataloging-in-Publication Data

Naeve, Milo M.
  Identifying American furniture : a pictorial guide to styles and terms, colonial to contemporary / Milo M. Naeve. — 2nd ed., rev. and expanded.
      p.   cm.
  Bibliography: p.
  Includes index.
    1. Furniture — United States — Styles. 2. Furniture — United States — Expertising.
I. Title.
NK2405.N28   1989   89-14923
749.213 — dc20   CIP

ISBN 0-393-30580-5

Cover photos show chronological style development of the desk/desk and bookcase. From text left to right: No. 18, pp. 8-9; No. 21, pp. 8-9; No. 24, pp. 10-11; No. 30, pp. 12-13; No. 40, pp. 14-15; and No. 125, pp. 46-47. *(Courtesy—The Art Institute of Chicago, Chicago, Illinois.)*

Contents

Introduction   vii

Preface   ix

Styles

Medieval Style, 1607-1700   3
Renaissance Style, 1607-1700   5
Restoration Style, 1660-1700   7
William and Mary Style, 1690-1730   9
Queen Anne Style, 1730-1760   11
Chippendale Style, 1755-1790   13
Federal Style, 1790-1815   15
Phyfe Style, 1801-1825   17
Classical Styles, 1805-1830   19
French Restauration Style, 1830-1850   21
Gothic Revival Style, 1840-1860   23
Elizabethan Style, 1850-1915   25
Rococo Revival Style, 1845-1870   27
Naturalistic Style, 1850-1865   29
Louis XVI Style, 1850-1914   31
Renaissance Revival Style, 1850-1880   33
Neo-Greek Style, 1855-1885   35
Egyptian Revival Style, 1865-1890   37
Reformed Gothic or Eastlake Style, 1870-1890   39
Art Furniture Styles, 1875-1914   41
Art Nouveau Style, 1896-1914   43
Arts and Crafts Styles, 1885-1915   45
Prairie School Style, 1900-1920   47

Art Deco Styles, 1925-1945   49
International Style, 1940-Present   51
Craftsman Styles, 1945-Present   53
Contemporary Styles, 1981-Present   55
Dutch Style, 1624-1860   57
German Style, 1750-1870   59
Spanish Style, 1600-1900   61
Vernacular Styles, 1670-1790   63
Vernacular Styles, 1791-1914   65
Shaker Style, 1800-1914   67
Windsor Style, 1750-Present   69
Garden Furniture Styles, 1800-1914   71

Further Reading

Periodicals   73
Books, Articles, and Manuscripts   73
  Background Sources: Architecture and Design   73
  General Sources: American Furniture   76
  Regional Sources: Hawaiian Islands   80
  Regional Sources: Mid-Atlantic   80
  Regional Sources: Midwest   82
  Regional Sources: New England   82
  Regional Sources: South   84
  Regional Sources: Southwest   85
  Regional Sources: West   85

Index   87

Introduction

Identifying American Furniture moves on the occasion of this edition to center stage in the intimate theater of publications by the American Association for State and Local History. There, it reverses the usual role of the actor receiving applause to applauding others. First among those deserving recognition are the readers of the first edition since 1981. They proved that a new edition is viable by making the first one the most widely sold publication by the Association. From another point of view, designers and craftsmen abruptly have opened a challenging new chapter in the history of American furniture and created a need for reporting it. Still others deserve mention for the imaginative inquiries which have brought many facets of our kaleidoscopic furniture history into sharper focus. Finally, it is a pleasure to express appreciation to the Association, which first realized the need for a concise handbook on American furniture, published it, and is now renewing the commitment with this edition.

I declined the opportunity for replacing my preface to the first edition because the observations there are as true now as the time written. But comment should be made here about a brief episode concerning the names of styles. An occasional interest in discarding them for the terms "Baroque" or "Early," "Mid- ," and "Late Colonial" has appeared and disappeared since 1981. The consensus is that those terms are even more vague than the traditional names.

Several styles are added to this edition. One is the Phyfe Style. It is separated from the Classical Styles because the furniture now is a subject of great interest and the name a subject of equally great confusion. Another addition is the Prairie School Style, which is drawn out of the Arts and Crafts Styles. Architectural historians long have recognized the distinct architectural personality of the upper Midwest at the dawn of the twentieth century, but the contemporary furniture only recently has gained a broad national and international public. Other changes from the first edition respond to innovative design since 1981. For this reason, the section formerly entitled "Craftsman and Contemporary Styles, 1945–Present" is divided into two parts. "Craftsman Styles" remains a survey since 1945, but "Contemporary Styles" reports since 1981.

Developments in recent years are matched by discoveries about our past. These have led to other changes in the text. Some dates are refined in the captions for objects, and happily the name of a designer or craftsman occasionally can be added. Publication of sound research has greatly extended the bibliography for background sources. There are even more additions to the entries for furniture made in the United States. They reveal that local furniture, including that of Hawaii, now is a strong interest in every region. Common to all of the recent publications is more precise documentation and broader analysis of influences on style. Some now obsolete entries in the first bibliography are omitted in this one, or their significance is defined in relation to recent publications on the same subject. The new bibliography, above all, responds to persistent requests for much more detailed guidance to studies about furniture in America or its sources abroad.

An interest in American furniture no longer is esoteric. While this concern continues, we shall remain in a stimulating era of discovery. I hope it forces future revisions of *Identifying American Furniture*.

MILO M. NAEVE

Field-McCormick Curator of American Arts
The Art Institute of Chicago

Preface

Styles in this handbook have swept nearly four centuries of designers, craftsmen, or patrons on the invisible winds of taste. They sometimes are an abrupt gale over a generation and sometimes a steady breeze over many.

I tried several times in several ways putting these constantly shifting and often elusive trends into a rational order in accordance with the first proposal for the project, made by Gary Gore, Director of Publications for the American Association for State and Local History. The Association wanted a succinct guide for identifying the style of a specific example, yet a broad survey for styles throughout our history. I declined.

The reasons are not mysterious. For one, the two objectives seemed contradictory. For another, I was greatly concerned at the time with very specific research on American paintings, and Gary's proposed project seemed to confirm a conclusion evident wherever curiosity erratically has led me, whether to the efforts of painters, sculptors, architects, silversmiths, potters, glassblowers, or cabinetmakers: our knowledge of the past is incomplete. It is formed by the accident of survival for documentary evidence and for works of art coupled with the even more whimsical chance encounter with either source. A responsible survey in a distilled form seemed unlikely.

The idea haunted me, however, because I often come across the need for the kind of publication that AASLH proposed. Finally, we agreed on the venture. Like all fine publishers, mine is also a gambler. Gary has proven my greatest ally, in giving complete freedom for translating his broad proposal into my specific approach. Our only foundation was that style, the appearance of furniture, is the most useful way of bringing clarity to a complex subject.

For that reason, the illustrations are the main elements of my survey. They are on the book's left-hand pages, for convenient reference, either for finding a style of interest or in comparing it with others for similarities or differences.

They are complemented in several ways. Superimposed numbers on each illustration identify stylistic elements that are listed on the right-hand page, with a brief essay about the style. The over-all number given to each picture (Fig. 1, Fig. 2, etc.) is a key to specific information in the illustration notes on the lower part of the right-hand page.

A selection of periodicals, books, and articles in the section titled "Further Reading" completes the book. This section offers resources for specific inquiries from several points of view.

The user of this guide will find that looking through the illustrations is often the best kind of index, but the usual sort is included, listing the number of the illustration where significant motifs, designers, craftsmen, manufacturers, materials, terms, and constructions may be found.

Styles, then, are defined in this survey by the illustrations. Each example is a fully developed expression, and, within a style, the selections offer elements that can be found in endless variations and combinations on other furniture. Elaborate interpretations of a style are emphasized, because their echo always remains in simplifications.

Especially before the mid-nineteenth century, styles evolved and lingered at different times in different places. My dates refer to the general period of popularity.

An individual would be best served, I decided, if all of the furniture in the guide were publicly available. Owners are identified with the illustrations, but the listed sources are only a few of the many possibilities available to the reader in the United States and in England. I urge complementing this guide with study of actual examples.

The greatest challenge in this survey has been to attain a balance between brevity and length. Styles have emerged in many different communities and areas that could be considered individually or treated as part of a broader trend. Most of my decisions are obvious. Others are personal, about the character of trends or the identification of trends that I believe will be useful to the greatest number of readers. There are, for example, separate categories for the Rococo Revival Style and the Naturalistic Style in the mid-nineteenth century: they are related, but they differ. The many interpretations of Neo-Classical motifs and forms in the early nineteenth century, as well as furniture in the Arts and Crafts styles in the early twentieth century and the later Art Deco styles, are placed in three general categories. Variations within these styles would be treated separately, in a detailed publication; but in this survey, they are grouped as expressions of general themes. What should be done with the styles of certain European immigrants? They often are the result of "folk" or "popular" culture, but I have separated them into Dutch, German, and Spanish traditions and excluded the distinctive French and Scandinavian furniture only because examples are few in number and less likely to concern the usual reader. Eccentric combinations of several styles are identified as "vernacular" styles, and examples were selected for demonstrating possibilities in the eighteenth and nineteenth centuries. I am uncomfortable with the term *vernacular*, which could refer to furniture in many degrees of simplification from sophisticated styles, but I prefer it to the inaccurate designation *country* and the vague one of *folk*. Windsor furniture may have originated with the generation of the Revolution, but it clearly is vital in our time, and I have taken the position of including a version with Windsors instead of Contemporary Styles.

My names for styles usually are those in common use. They originated over the last century, with the revival of designs from earlier periods and with an analytical approach to the history of furniture. Inconsistencies occur in references to political periods, design sources, craftsmen, religious or national groups, and international exhibitions, but the names have the advantage of general familiarity.

American furniture rarely can be mistaken for furniture made abroad, but Americans from the seventeenth century to the present have continued the international tradition of style launched by Greeks borrowing from Egyptians and Romans from Greeks. Among many influences, English taste prevailed through the seventeenth and eighteenth centuries, English and French in the nineteenth, and French and German in the twentieth. European books and magazines directly pertinent to the evolution of American styles are mentioned in the commentaries. Their significance is documented, but equally pertinent and rarely known specifically are the influences of immigrant craftsmen, imported furniture and patrons traveling abroad.

Technology is considered in this guide only when essential to the visual features of style. At times, technology served craftsmen with better ways of manipulating materials or achieving decorative effects. At other times, it gave craftsmen such new materials as plastics. The influence of technology, however, should not be overestimated. An innovation, such as laminated woods, might be introduced in the mid-nineteenth century and ignored until the mid-twentieth.

The advantage of a summary in a handbook of this nature bears the counterweight disadvantage of omission. Illustrations and text within these covers survey only major movements in domestic furniture. Many forms before the nineteenth century, especially bedsteads, have not survived for documenting styles completely. Innovative styles in the twentieth century are stressed over commercial adaptations and reproductions of historic styles, which are a fascinating dimension in cultural history but derivative in form and decoration.

A survey with a different accent could be published within a decade, if designers of contemporary furniture and researchers into the past continue their current vitality. But I believe my broad scheme is true now and will remain so for all who respond to the fascination of stylistic change through the years.

Styles

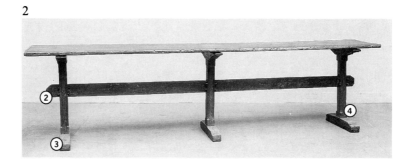

Medieval Style, 1607-1700

English medieval traditions continue in New England and in the South through ordinary furniture in houses as sparsely furnished as those abroad. There is greater evidence for the appearance of storage and seating furniture than for bedsteads, settles, or livery cupboards.

The popular slab-ended chest is made of five pine boards nailed together, with sides extended as feet and a sixth board used as the pinned or hinged top. Decoration includes incised, punched, or painted geometric designs in red, black, and white. The form occurs in England by the fourteenth century and continues in New England through the early nineteenth.

Storage boxes are as simply made and decorated as chests. Some include chip carving, known in England by the thirteenth century.

Armchairs and side chairs with rush or splint seats and turned spindles, legs, and arms differ in design and kinds of woods used from New England to the South. These types of chairs occur as early as the eleventh century in England, but the usual English and American seat during the seventeenth century is the stool.

New England furniture includes a medieval type of table with a removable top and stretcher on trestles. A version with a fixed top and stretcher continues to the early nineteenth century.

1. **Turned spindles**
2. **Stretcher**
3. **Chamfer**
4. **Trestle base**
5. **Splint seat**
6. **Moldings**
7. **Cleat**
8. **Finial**
9. **Chip carving**
10. **Egg-and-dart motif (Renaissance Style)**

1. Armchair (Great chair), Connecticut, 1670-1710; ash. *The Art Institute of Chicago, Wirt D. Walker Fund, Chicago, Illinois.*

2. Table, New England, 1640-1670; pine top, oak base. *The Metropolitan Museum of Art, gift of Mrs. Russell Sage, 1909, New York, New York.*

3. Armchair (Great chair), Virginia or North Carolina, 1690-1720; maple, oak. *The Museum of Early Southern Decorative Arts, Winston-Salem, North Carolina.*

4. Six-board chest, Connecticut or Massachusetts, 1671-1710; pine. *Yale University Art Gallery, The Mabel Brady Garvan Collection, New Haven, Connecticut.*

5. Highchair for child, probably Dorchester, Massachusetts, 1636-1670; silver maple. *The Art Institute of Chicago, gift of Elizabeth R. Vaughan, Chicago, Illinois.*

6. Box, New Hampshire, 1674-1700; white pine. *The Art Institute of Chicago, gift of Marshall Field, Mrs. C. Phillip Miller, and Mrs. Frank L. Sulzberger, Chicago, Illinois.*

7

8

9

10

11

Renaissance Style, 1607-1700

Rectilinear oak forms with boldly curved elements and massive turnings are accented with relief carving against black, white, green, and red backgrounds. Survivals in the style of somber Renaissance splendor mainly are from New England.

Joiners secured parts with wooden pins or nailed bottom and backboards. Chests and boxes are common among the limited forms. Seating includes joint stools—a reference to joined construction—and chair-tables with backs lowering for table tops. Court cupboards offer a bottom shelf below a recessed cupboard; press cupboards are a variation with compartments enclosing the lower section. Tables occasionally include leaves, either drawing outward or opening onto a moveable leg. Evidence is limited for bedsteads, but they probably were similar to the nineteenth-century vernacular form, and elaborate versions apparently included posts.

The Renaissance Style originated in rural England from continental versions of the Italian Renaissance. Revived from Roman art are acanthus leaves and flowers, Doric columns, Roman arches, and torus, scotia, and astragal moldings. They merge with Renaissance circular and round feet, channel moldings, bands of notches and triangles, bulbous turnings, lunettes, foliage, attenuated leaves, bosses, grotesques, lozenges, and strapwork. Spindles, cut in half, glued together, turned, and broken apart form the common decoration known as "split spindles."

1. Finial (Restoration)
2. Strapwork
3. Relief carving
4. Grotesque
5. Foliate scroll
6. Doric column
7. Collarino
8. Split spindle
9. Lozenge
10. Boss
11. Cleat
12. Stile
13. Rail
14. Stipple background or carved panel
15. Lunette
16. Muntin
17. Leaf design
18. Wooden pins for a mortise-and-tenon joint
19. Channel molding
20. Apron or skirt
21. Astragal or bead molding
22. Ball foot variation

7. Armchair (Great chair), attributed to Thomas Dennis, Ipswich, Massachusetts, 1668-1675; oak. *The Essex Institute, Salem, Massachusetts.*

8. Joint stool, attributed to Stephen Jaques, Newbury, Massachusetts, 1680-1710; red oak. *The Henry Francis du Pont Winterthur Museum, Winterthur, Delaware.*

9. Press cupboard, attributed to the Emery Shops, Newbury, Massachusetts, 1675-1695; oak, pine. *The Museum of Fine Arts, Boston, gift of Maurice Geeraerts,* *in memory of Mr. and Mrs. William R. Robeson, Boston, Massachusetts.*

10. Chest, Plymouth, Massachusetts, area, 1641 (dated); white oak, pine top. *The Art Institute of Chicago, Elizabeth R. Vaughan Fund, Chicago, Illinois.*

11. Table, Massachusetts, 1660-1690; oak. *The Wadsworth Atheneum, Wallace Nutting Collection, gift of J. P. Morgan, Hartford, Connecticut.*

12

13

14

15

16

Restoration Style, 1660-1700

Comforts and conveniences still known today are introduced in new forms featuring upholstery in couches, side chairs, or armchairs, drawers in tables, chests of drawers or high chests, and tables with hinged leaves supported on gate-legs. Design and decoration of these forms shift radically from rectilinear simplicity at the close of the austere British Commonwealth in 1659 to Baroque curves with restoration of the monarchy and luxury. Innovations in form and decoration reached New England and the Middle Colonies over the late seventeenth century, often influenced the Renaissance Style, and merged into the later William and Mary Style.

Oak is commonly used, but walnut and maple better serve the new fashions. Turnings range from round or oval shapes to discs or spirals. Feet are circular, round, or oval. Geometric panels on case furniture or drawers are framed by classical moldings or wide bevels against a field in light and dark woods, black and red paint, or grained patterns.

1. **Cleat**
2. **Split spindle**
3. **Black paint**
4. **Owner initials**
5. **Reel turning**
6. **Ball foot variation**
7. **Cyma reversa molding**
8. **Astragal molding**
9. **Ovolo molding**
10. **Spiral turned spindles**
11. **Recessed seat for cushion**
12. **Stretchers(front, back, side, medial)**
13. **Bevel**
14. **Boss**
15. **Leather upholstery with brass tacks**
16. **Velvet cushion**
17. **Ball turning**

12. Chamber table, Essex County, Massachusetts, 1670-1690; oak. *The Art Institute of Chicago, Sewell L. Avery Fund, Chicago, Illinois.*

13. High chest of drawers, New York, 1680-1700; gumwood. *The Metropolitan Museum of Art, Rogers Fund, 1936, New York, New York.*

14. Side chair, Philadelphia, Pennsylvania, or Burlington, New Jersey, 1690-1700; walnut. *The Philadelphia Museum of Art; purchased by subscription and museum funds, Philadelphia, Pennsylvania.*

15. Chest of drawers, Massachusetts, 1660-1690; oak, pine. *The Shelburne Museum, Shelburne, Vermont.*

16. Armchair, Boston, Massachusetts, 1660-1665; oak, maple. *The Museum of Fine Arts, Boston, Seth K. Sweetster Fund, Boston, Massachusetts.*

17

18

19

20

21

22

William and Mary Style, 1690-1730

Taut curves and crisp rectangles create dynamic tension in the style identified with the English monarch William of Orange and his consort Mary. Case furniture is reduced to crisp planes, and the facade often is decorated with boldly grained walnut or maple veneers framed by inlaid bands. Classical moldings are exaggerated in size. Baluster-shaped turnings and C-shaped scrolls create rippling movement. Feet usually are round or oval. An alternate foot — known as "Portuguese," paintbrush, or "Spanish" — flares into a scroll. Case furniture may be decorated with imitation lacquer know as japanning, which continues in the Queen Anne and Chippendale styles (No. 26).

Gate-leg tables and high chests are common forms originating with the Restoration Style. High and narrow backs are upholstered, caned, or, in simple furniture, fitted with spindles turned and split in the manner of the Renaissance Style. Other forms are daybeds, dressing tables repeating the bases of high chests, side tables, easy chairs and desks with an occasional upper section fitted as a bookcase. Tea tables and tall case clocks are introduced, but are rare.

The Continental Baroque, with a new emphasis on classicism, determined the style. It was encouraged by the king, his Huguenot designer Daniel Marot, and immigrant Dutch and French craftsmen.

1. Spanish, Portuguese, or paintbrush foot
2. Velvet upholstery
3. Horizontally rolled arm
4. Vertically rolled arm support
5. Medial stretcher with double ball-and-ring turnings
6. Loper (supports hinged lid)
7. Slide for candlestick (each side)
8. Hinged door with fielded panel
9. Cornice
10. Pediment with hood
11. Urn-shaped finial
12. Double astragal or bead molding
13. Ball-shaped foot
14. Crest with volutes, leaf carving, and C scrolls matches stretcher
15. Finial with ball-over-urn shape
16. Tuscan columnar-turned stile
17. Baluster turning
18. Leather back panel and seat upholstery with brass tacks
19. Stretchers (side, medial, rear)
20. Cavetta molding
21. Cyma reversa molding
22. Flitches of walnut veneer
23. Pendant or drop
24. Stretchers match skirt shape
25. Walnut veneer over facade
26. Star, or compass, inlay
27. Herringbone banding
28. Cyma molding
29. Drawer with knob handle
30. Gate-leg (each side) supports hinged leaf
31. Double baluster turning

17. Easy chair, probably Boston, Massachusetts, 1715-1730; maple. *The Museum of Fine Arts, Houston, the Bayou Bend Collection, gift of Miss Ima Hogg, Houston, Texas.*

18. Desk and bookcase, Boston, Massachusetts, 1701-1735; walnut, white pine. *The Art Institute of Chicago, gift of the Antiquarian Society through the Mr. and Mrs. William Y. Hutchinson Fund, Chicago, Illinois.*

19. Armchair, Boston, Massachusetts, 1695-1710; maple, oak. *The Henry Francis du Pont Winterthur Museum, Winterthur, Delaware.*

20. High chest of drawers, New York, 1690-1725; walnut, Southern yellow pine, cedar. *The Art Institute of Chicago, gift of Jamee J. Field and Marshall Field, Chicago, Illinois.*

21. Desk (*scrutoir*), probably Boston, Massachusetts, 1690-1720; walnut, white pine. *The Art Institute of Chicago, gift of the Antiquarian Society through Joyce Martin Brown, Lena T. Gilbert, Mrs. Harold T. Martin, and Melinda Martin Vance, Chicago, Illinois.*

22. Table, Massachusetts, 1710-1730; walnut, white pine. *The Art Institute of Chicago, gift of Mr. and Mrs. William Salisbury, Chicago, Illinois.*

23

24

25

26

27

28

Queue Anne Style, 1730-1760

Queen Anne Style curves revolutionize form in cabriole legs, pediments, and aprons, or splats, crests, and arms of chairs. Curves recur in scallop shells carved on legs, chair crest rails, or drawers.

Boston, Newport, New York, and Philadelphia are centers of regional variations. Stretchers occur on chairs, and forms are attenuated in New England. Construction differs; in Philadelphia, for example, chair rails are mortised through the back legs of chairs. New England favors pad feet and Pennsylvania trifid feet. Furniture in Rhode Island, Connecticut, New York, and Pennsylvania occasionally includes slipper and claw-and-ball feet.

Popular forms are rectangular tea tables, gate-leg tables, desks, high chests, dressing tables, and side chairs or easy chairs. Settees, sofas, couches, armchairs, desks and bookcases, and tall clocks are rare. Bedsteads with low posts are common; many occur with high posts, and cabriole legs with pad feet appear on elaborate versions. Tea tables are introduced with a circular tilting top. Card tables occur with a hinged top supported on a gate-leg. Chests of drawers are rare.

The style evolved in Queen Anne's court (1702-1714) and survived to the Revolution. Walnut is popular, cherry and maple are common, and late versions of the style are in mahogany. Japanned decoration in red, green and gilt usually is on a blue-green field. The style has inspired innovative design in the 1980s (No. 146).

1. **Applied molding**
2. **Skirt pendant**
3. **Collarino**
4. **Pointed slipper foot (mainly Rhode Island and New York)**
5. **Scrolled, or broken-arch, pediment**
6. **Urn-shaped finial**
7. **Inlaid band**
8. **Mirrored glass panel on hinged door (each side)**
9. **Pilaster**
10. **Slide for candlestick**
11. **Loper (supports hinged lid)**
12. **Block front design (mainly New England)**
13. **Bracket foot (restoration)**
14. **Crest rail with yoke (New England type)**
15. **Curved shoulder (Newport type)**
16. **Splat (New England type)**
17. **Shoe**
18. **Compass (shape) slip seat with upholstery**
19. **Seat rail with shaped front**
20. **Cabriole leg**
21. **Pad foot (mainly New England)**
22. **Shaped medial and side stretchers (mainly Rhode Island)**
23. **Astragal, or bead, molding**
24. **Chamfered corners**
25. **Cyma reversa molding**
26. **Carved and gilded scallop shell above festoon**
27. **Japanned decoration**
28. **Pendant or drop**
29. **Lion paw foot (rare)**
30. **Tester**
31. **Bedstead (wooden framework)**
32. **Headboard**
33. **Columnar footposts**
34. **Shaped front and side skirts**
35. **Knee bracket**
36. **Disc below turned pad foot**

23. Tea table, Newport, Rhode Island, 1740-1760; mahogany. *The Art Institute of Chicago, gift of Sewell L. Avery, Emily Crane Chadbourne, Miss Heath-Jones, Ellen Lamotte, Charles F. Montgomery, Mr. and Mrs. John Trumbull, Russell Tyson, Elizabeth R. Vaughan, and The Wirt D. Walker Fund, Chicago, Illinois.*

24. Desk and bookcase, Boston, Massachusetts, 1735-1750; mahogany with oak and white pine secondary woods. *The Art Institute of Chicago, Major Acquisitions Centennial Fund, Chicago, Illinois.*

25. Side chair, Rhode Island, 1730-1760; walnut. *The Art Institute of Chicago, Robert Allerton Fund, Chicago, Illinois.*

26. High chest of drawers; John Pimm, cabinetmaker, with japanning possibly by Thomas Johnson, Boston, Massachusetts, 1740-1750; maple, pine. *The Henry Francis du Pont Winterthur Museum, Winterthur, Delaware.*

27. Bed, Rhode Island or Massachusetts, 1740-1760; mahogany and maple. *The Henry Francis du Pont Winterthur Museum, Winterthur, Delaware.*

28. Dressing table, Essex County, Massachusetts, 1750-1770; mahogany, white pine. *The Art Institute of Chicago, gift of the Antiquarian Society through Mrs. Wiiliam O. Hunt, Jessie Spalding Landon, Mrs. Harold T. Martin, Adelaide Ryerson, and Melinda Martin Vance, Chicago, Illinois.*

Chinese frets, Gothic arches and quatrefoils, *C*- and *S*-shaped scrolls, ribbons, flowers, leaves, scallop shells, and other French rococo motifs occur with gadrooning, acanthus leaves, columns, capitals, and moldings from Roman architecture. The Chippendale Style is identified today with the English cabinetmaker Thomas Chippendale, whose *Gentleman and Cabinet-Makers Director*—a book of furniture designs published in 1754, 1755, and 1762 in London—nourished the style in England and America.

Mahogany is popular, and walnut, maple, or cherry occur in forms of the Queen Anne Style carved with diverse ornament. Chest of drawers, fire screens, and looking glasses are fashionable. Straight legs replace the cabriole late in the period, ogee bracket feet are popular, and Marlborough feet are favored in Pennsylvania. Japanning is frequent.

Charleston is a new center of craftsmanship among those continuing from the Queen Anne Style. Regional preference in New England include stretchers on chairs and concave and convex panels known as blocking. The bombé form appears mainly in Boston. Five legs instead of four occur on card tables in New York, and the shape of claw-and-ball feet varies significantly. Philadelphians make the most elaborate furniture in shops organized in the London manner with specialists.

1. Hinged top
2. Applied carved gadrooning
3. *C* scroll
4. Gate-leg (fifth leg: New York only)
5. Claw-and-ball foot (New York type)
6. Cabriole leg
7. Ogee bracket foot
8. Block-front design (mainly New England)
9. Classical wave pattern
10. Loper
11. Crest rail
12. Splat with lozenge, volutes, and *C* scrolls
13. Fluted stile
14. Shoe
15. Side rail
16. Front rail
17. Bracket
18. Acanthus leaf carving
19. Claw-and-ball foot (Philadelphia type)
20. Finial (Philadelphia type)
21. Cornice
22. Applied Rococo leaf carving
23. Face (dial and spandrels)
24. Fluted Doric column
25. Indented fluted quarter-column
26. Scrolled, or broken-arch, pediment
27. Rosette
28. Chamfered and fluted corner
29. Scallop shell
30. Shaped apron or skirt
31. Bombé form
32. Serpentine curve
33. Claw-and-ball foot (Massachusetts type)

29. Gaming table, New York, 1755-1790; mahogany, poplar, oak. *The Art Institute of Chicago, gift of Robert Allerton, Bessie Bennett, Mr. and Mrs. Robert Brown, Annie Dunlap Estate, in memory of Annie Wisner, and Mrs. Potter Palmer, Chicago, Illinois.*

30. Desk, probably Norwich, Connecticut, 1755-1805; mahogany, white pine. *The Art Institute of Chicago, gift of the Antiquarian Society through Jessie Spalding Landon, Chicago, Illinois.*

31. Side chair, Philadelphia, Pennsylvania, 1755-1765; mahogany. *The Art Institute of Chicago, gift of the Robert R. McCormick Charitable Trust, Chicago, Illinois.*

32. Clock, Philadelphia, Pennsylvania, 1755-1790. *Greenfield Village and Henry Ford Museum, Dearborn, Michigan. (Accession No. 00.3.8929.)*

33. High chest of drawers, probably Maryland, 1755-1790; mahogany, yellow pine, poplar, cedar. *The Art Institute of Chicago, gift of the Antiquarian Society, Chicago, Illinois.*

34. Bureau table, attributed to John Townsend, Newport, Rhode Island, 1765-1775; mahogany with maple, chestnut, and white pine. *The Art Institute of Chicago, gift of Jamee J. and Marshall Field, Chicago, Illinois.*

35. Chest of drawers, Boston, Massachusetts, 1770-1795; mahogany, white pine. *The Art Institute of Chicago, the Helen Bowen Blair Fund, Chicago, Illinois.*

36

37

38

40

39

41

Federal Style, 1790-1815

Mahogany forms veneered with mahogany, maple, birch, or satinwood are severe, with straight, oval, and serpentine lines. Decoration is inlaid, carved, or occasionally painted. Motifs are Roman bellflowers, paterae, urns, festoons, flutes, acanthus leaves, and pilasters with such contemporary elements as shields, Prince of Wales feathers, or eagles representing both Rome and the new nation. Rococo curves, flowers, and ribbons or Gothic arches and quatrefoils are occasional. Accents are inlaid lines or bands. Straight legs taper in planes or are circular in cross-section with reeding. Feet often are bulbous turnings or tapered spades.

Chippendale forms continue with new delicacy. They include stands, card tables, dining tables, and Pembroke tables. Sofas, settees, and chairs occur in variety. Sideboards and work tables are introduced.

Robert Adam orginated the English style during the 1760s, and it reached the United States by 1790. English pattern books are influential. One is Alice Hepplewhite's *The Cabinet-Maker and Upholsterer's Guide* (1788; 1789; 1794). Others by Thomas Sheraton are *The Cabinet-Maker and Upholsterer's Drawing-Book* (1791-1794; 1802), *The Cabinet Dictionary* (1803), and *The Cabinet-Maker, Upholsterer, and General Artist's Encyclopedia* (1804-1806).

1. **Shield-shaped back**
2. **Carved drapery festoon**
3. **Urn**
4. **Spade foot**
5. **Serpentine shape**
6. **Inlaid flutes**
7. **Inlaid patera**
8. **Inlaid husks**
9. **Serpentine curve**
10. **Reeding**
11. **Satinwood veneer**
12. **Knurling**
13. **Work bag (access through false drawer)**
14. **Inlaid urn**
15. **Stringing (inlaid bands)**
16. **Castor**
17. **Finial**
18. **Muntin**
19. **Inlaid pilaster**
20. **Birch veneer**
21. **Cornice**
22. **Loper**
23. **Hinged top**

36. Side chair, carving attributed to Samuel McIntire, Salem, Massachusetts, 1795-1811; mahogany. *The Art Institute of Chicago, gift of the Antiquarian Society through Edith Almy Adams, Chicago, Illinois.*

37. Sideboard, New York City area, 1790-1815; mahogany, white pine, poplar, oak. *The Art Institute of Chicago, gift of the Antiquarian Society through Mrs. Clive Runnells, Chicago, Illinois.*

38. Work table, Salem, Massachusetts, 1793-1814; mahogany with satinwood and white pine. *The Art Institute of Chicago, gift of the Antiquarian Society through Susan and Richard M. Bennett, Chicago, Illinois.*

39. Pembroke table, New York City area, 1795-1810; mahogany. *The Art Institute of Chicago, gift of the Illinois District Chapter of the American Institute of Interior Designers and Emily Crane Chadbourne, Chicago, Illinois.*

40. Desk and bookcase, New Hampshire, 1800-1815; mahogany and birch veneers, white pine. *The Art Institute of Chicago, gift of Mr. and Mrs. Robert Sack, Chicago, Illinois.*

41. Card table, Royal H. Gould, Chester, Vermont, 1816-1830; cherry with maple veneer. *The Art Institute of Chicago, restricted gift of Mrs. Burton W. Hales, Chicago, Illinois.*

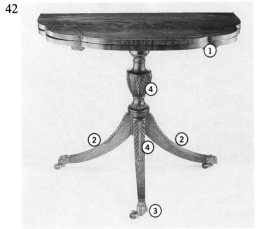

42

43

44

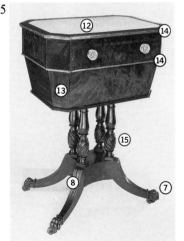

45

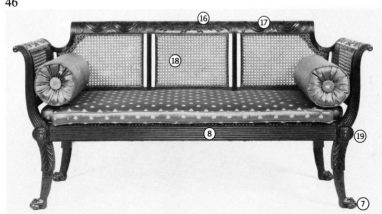

46

47

Phyfe Style, 1801-1825

No American cabinetmaker is as well known as Duncan Phyfe (1768-1854). His fame was born in his own time, for documents by contemporaries identify their furniture as conforming to Phyfe's style.

Characteristics of it are fine mahogany, excellence in craftsmanship, and restraint in design. Phyfe did not invent the forms or motifs; he adapted them from contemporary English furniture and design books. Significant among his sources is the *London Chair-Maker's and Carver's Book of Prices for Workmanship* first issued in 1802 and reprinted with a supplement in 1808.

Phyfe originally had emigrated from Scotland, where he was trained, to Albany. He was living in New York City by 1792 and developed his firm with the extraordinary growth of the city. He eventually managed about 150 employees, in contrast to most contemporary firms with less than 12, and probably 3-6, workers. Phyfe not only dominated the craft in his adopted city, but he also sold furniture in the coastal trade to the South. As his firm developed, Phyfe became more of an executive than a craftsman.

Very little furniture can be securely identified with Phyfe's shop through labels, bills, or histories of ownership. Attributions cannot at present be made on the basis of carved motifs, general designs, or construction because employees often moved between shops, and owners subcontracted work among themselves and to such specialists as carvers or turners.

Phyfe's style is an enduring one. Craftsmen revived it and even forged it with the concern for antique furniture in the late nineteenth century. Manufacturers have continued this style through the twentieth century. Later in his career Phyfe adopted other styles (Nos. 57, 58), which are not identified with his name.

1. **Triple elliptic front**
2. **Back legs rotate when top opened**
3. **Brass lion foot**
4. **Leaf carving**
5. **Lyre-shaped splat**
6. **Slip seat**
7. **Carved lion foot**
8. **Reeding**
9. **Elliptic front**
10. **Typical turned shape in New York City**
11. **Carved dog foot**
12. **Marble top**
13. **Canted corner**
14. **Brass band**
15. **Whorled baluster**
16. **Carved cornucopia**
17. **Carved swags**
18. **Caning**
19. **Carved lion face**
20. **Motif of carved reeds tied with bowknot**
21. **Rosette**

42. Card table, Phyfe Style, New York City, 1810-1820; mahogany. *The Henry Francis du Pont Winterthur Museum, Winterthur, Delaware.*

43. Side chair, Phyfe Style, New York City, 1810-1820; mahogany. *The Henry Francis du Pont Winterthur Museum, Winterthur, Delaware.*

44. Chest of drawers, Phyfe Style, New York City, 1810-1820; mahogany, tulip, and white pine. *The Henry Francis du Pont Winterthur Museum, Winterthur, Delaware.*

45. Work table, Duncan Phyfe Shop (documented by label), New York City, 1815-1816; mahogany, tulip, white pine. *The Henry Francis du Pont Winterthur Museum, Winterthur, Delaware.*

46. Settee, Phyfe Style, New York City, 1810-1820; mahogany. *The Art Institute of Chicago, Robert Allerton Fund, Chicago, Illinois.*

47. Armchair, Duncan Phyfe Shop (documented by bill), New York City, 1807; mahogany. *The Henry Francis du Pont Winterthur Museum, Winterthur, Delaware.*

Classical Styles, 1805-1830

Dog or lion feet, anthemia, and other motifs adopting the form of couches and *klismos* chairs revive the classical world with a Grecian emphasis (No. 52).

Sofa tables, parlor tables, French secretaries, and wardrobes are new forms. New designs appear for beds, card tables, sideboards, and sofas.

Carved decoration in the principal wood of mahogany often is painted black or gilded. Inlaid lines may occur in ebony and veneers in maple. Ormolu is common and imitated with gilt stenciling.

The American eagle is among occasional motifs. Motifs from Egyptian art are popularized by Napoleon's campaigns and Nelson's victories. Gothic influence occurs in pointed arches and quatrefoils.

Diverse designs reveal the continuity of English influence and a direct relationship with France. Significant English publications are cabinetmakers' guides, Thomas Hope's *Household Furniture* of 1807, George Smith's *Household Furniture* of 1808, and Rudolph Ackermann's *Repository of Arts*. Influential French publications are Pierre de la Mésangère's *Collections des muebles et objets de goût* and the 1801 and 1812 editions of Charles Percier and Pierre F. L. Fontaine's *Recuil de decorations intérieures*.

New York City becomes the center of fashion and furniture production. Regional variations occur elsewhere.

1. **Ormolu**
2. **Satinwood veneer**
3. **Dolphin-shaped foot**
4. **Hinged top**
5. **Brass inlay**
6. **Sphinx**
7. **Gilt wood**
8. **Lion paw-shaped feet**
9. **Mahogany veneer**
10. **Canted corner**
11. **Cornice**
12. **Acanthus leaf**
13. **Gothic (lancet) arch muntin**
14. **Anthemion**
15. **Gadrooning**
16. ***Klismos* chair adaptation**
17. **Astragal molding**
18. **Palmette**
19. **Rosette**
20. **Slip seat with original upholstery foundation**
21. **Haircloth upholstery**
22. **Reeding**
23. **Castor with eagle design**
24. **Cornucopia-shaped leg**

48. Bedstead, Charles-Honoré Lannuier, New York City, circa 1817; mahogany with satinwood veneer. *The Albany Institute of History and Art, gift of Mrs. William Dexter, Albany, New York.*

49. Card table, Charles-Honoré Lannuier, New York City, circa 1817; mahogany. *The Albany Institute of History and Art, gift of Stephen Van Rensselaer Crosby, Albany, New York.*

50. Piano, James Stewart, Baltimore, Maryland, 1818; mahogany. *The Art Institute of Chicago, gift of Mrs. Herbert P. McLaughlin, Chicago, Illinois.*

51. Desk and bookcase, Antoine Gabriel Quervelle, Philadelphia, Pennsylvania, circa 1835; mahogany. *The Munson-Williams-Proctor Institute, Utica, New York.*

52. Side chair, Sherlock Spooner and George Trask, Boston, Massachusetts, 1825-1826; mahogany with white pine slip seat frame. *The Art Institute of Chicago, restricted gift of Mrs. Harold T. Martin, Chicago, Illinois.*

53. Grecian couch, New England, 1810-1835; mahogany, birch, white pine. *The Art Institute of Chicago, gift of Joseph P. Antonow, Chicago, Illinois.*

54

55

56

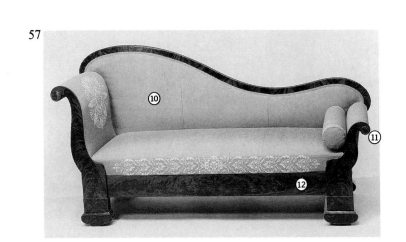

57

58

French Restauration Style, 1830-1850

Simplicity, practicality, and comfort mark the French Restauration Style. Born in France, it evolved during restoration of the Bourbons to the throne, from 1814 to 1848. Undulating curves balance geometric forms. Plain surfaces are relieved by spare ornament. The style includes the Egyptian lotus, circles, ormolu, and such simple moldings as the astragal, or bead. White marble and particularly the rich color and grain of mahogany veneers are significant to this style.

Forms often are conservative versions of the late Classical Style. Card tables retain the single pedestal, sofas an asymmetrical shape, and stools the curule form. Chairs are inspired by the *klismos* shape in Classical Greece, but they typically are transformed by curves in the crest, urn-shaped splats, braces curved from crest to seat, and the shape of legs.

Simplicity of the French Restauration Style encouraged interpretations over a long period in large and small centers of craftsmanship from Boston to New Orleans. Pierre de la Mésangère's Parisian periodical *Collection de meubles et objects de goût* recorded the style in France; George Smith's *Cabinet-Maker and Upholsterer's Guide,* published in 1826 in London, offered the English variation; and John Hall's *The Cabinet Makers Assistant,* published in 1840 in Baltimore, recorded a version in the United States.

1. **Curved and concave crest rail**
2. **Urn-shaped splat**
3. **Cabriole leg**
4. **Hinged top**
5. **Central pedestal support**
6. **Scroll foot**
7. **Castor**
8. **Red leather upholstery**
9. **Ormolu**
10. **Linen and wool rep upholstery**
11. **Concentric circle motif**
12. **Mahogany veneer**
13. **Marble top**
14. **Mirror**
15. **Canted corner**

54. Side chair (*chaise gondole*), probably New Orleans, Louisiana, 1835-1850; mahogany. *The Museum of Fine Arts, Houston, the Bayou Bend Collection, gift of Miss Ima Hogg, Houston, Texas.*

55. Card table, New York City, 1835-1845; mahogany. *The New-York Historical Society, New York, New York.*

56. Library chair, probably New York City, 1830-1840; mahogany. *Historic Hudson Valley, Sunnyside, Tarrytown, New York.*

57. Daybed (*méridienne*), attributed to Duncan Phyfe, New York City, 1837; mahogany. *The Metropolitan Museum of Art, L. E. Katzenbach Foundation gift, 1966, New York, New York.*

58. Pier table, attributed to Duncan Phyfe, New York City, 1830-1840; mahogany with marble top. *The Metropolitan Museum of Art, Edgar J. Kaufmann, Jr., Charitable Foundation Fund, 1968, New York, New York.*

59

60

61

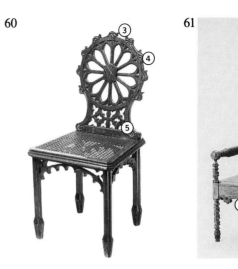

62

63

64

Gothic Revival Style, 1840-1860

Pointed arches, trefoils, quatrefoils, tracery, crockets, Tudor roses, and clustered columns from the architectural style common in western Europe between the twelfth and the sixteenth centuries are adapted to mid–nineteenth-century furniture forms. Among them the étagère, or whatnot, and dining tables extended by mechanical parts are newly popular.

Medieval furniture forms are not reproduced. They were generally unrecognized in a period of vague historical knowledge, and those known did not meet the comforts and needs of contemporary life.

Walnut and oak are common woods, with occasional use of mahogany and rosewood. Furniture ranges from large-in-scale to small; silhouettes are bold; carved details accent plain surfaces.

English fashion inspired the Gothic Revival Style. It never gained the popularity it held abroad, but the motifs had been a consistent theme since the mid–eighteenth-century Chippendale Style.

Contemporaries also knew the Gothic Revival Style as *Norman* and *Medieval.* Motifs mingle with those of the Restauration Style in an early phase and later with motifs of the Rococo Revival Style. Significant books offering designs are A. W. Pugin's *Gothic Furniture in the Style of the Fifteenth Century,* published in London in 1835, and Robert Conner's *Cabinet Makers Assistant,* published in New York City in 1842.

1. **Machine banding**
2. **Octagonal column**
3. **Wheel-shaped back**
4. **Crocket**
5. **Trefoil**
6. **Finial**
7. **Trefoil arch**
8. **Quatrefoil**
9. **Pendant or drop**
10. **Ogee arch**
11. **Roman arch**
12. **Cluster column**
13. **Maple veneer**
14. **Plinth**
15. **Lancet arch**
16. **Mirror**
17. **Marble**
18. **Castor**

59. Extension dining table, New York City, 1842-1845; mahogany. *The Munson-Williams-Proctor Institute, gift of Mrs. Erving Pruyn, Utica, New York.*

60. Side chair, designed by Alexander Jackson Davis, probably 1841, made by Richard Byrne, Dobbs Ferry, New York, or Ambrose Wright, Hastings (now Hastings-on-Hudson), New York, circa 1842; oak. *Lyndhurst, a property of the National Trust for Historic Preservation, Tarrytown, New York.*

61. Armchair, New York City, 1841-1850; oak. *The Art Institute of Chicago, restricted gift of Jeffrey Shedd, Chicago, Illinois.*

62. Chest of drawers and mirror, United States, circa 1846-1866; walnut, maple. *The Smithsonian Institution, the National Museum of History and Technology, Washington, D.C., gift of the city of Bridgeport, Connecticut.*

63. Étagère, probably New York City, 1845-1855; rosewood with marble top. *The Brooklyn Museum, H. Randolph Lever Fund, New York, New York.*

64. Settee, attributed to Thomas Brooks, Brooklyn, New York, circa 1846; walnut, cherry. *The Society for the Preservation of New England Antiquities, Boston, Massachusetts.*

65

66

67

68

69

Elizabethan Style, 1850-1915

Ball and spiral turnings, strapwork, and flowers with leaves are features of the Elizabethan Style. Less popular in America than in England, it is mainly confined in the United States to chairs in walnut, mahogany, or rosewood, and to informal painted bedroom suites known as "cottage furniture."

The period of greatest popularity was at mid-century. Vague historical knowledge wrongly credited many motifs and chairs with high backs to the reign of Queen Elizabeth, instead of correctly assigning them to the Restoration and the William and Mary styles of England.

The Elizabethan Style frequently mingled with the contemporary Rococo Revival and is a variant of the Renaissance Revival Style, based on English instead of continental sources. It lingered through the late nineteenth and early twentieth centuries as an accent for rooms furnished in other styles.

Walter Scott's novels during the 1820s influenced concern for the "Elizabethan" period, as did Henry Shaw's investigation of English antique furniture titled *Specimens of Ancient Furniture,* published in London in 1836. Robert Bridgen's influential designs for this style appeared in his *Furniture with Candelabra and Interior Decoration,* published in London in 1838.

1. Inlay
2. Baluster turning
3. Adaptation of strapwork design
4. Fluting
5. Split spindle
6. Spiral Turning
7. Needlework upholstery
8. Stretchers (front, back, side, medial)
9. Claw-and-ball foot
10. Ball turning
11. Castor

65. Side chair, Herter Brothers, New York City, 1869; rosewood. From the LeGrand Lockwood house, Norwalk, Connecticut. *The Art Institute of Chicago, Wesley M. Dixon, Jr. Fund, Chicago, Illinois.*

66. Chest of drawers and mirror, probably New York City, circa 1850; painted pine. *Historic Hudson Valley, Sunnyside, Tarrytown, New York.*

67. Side chair, probably New York City, circa 1851-1861; rosewood, mahogany. *The Museum of the City of New York, gift of Mrs. Henry De Bevoise Schenck, New York, New York.*

68. Armchair, United States, 1890-1900; mahogany. *The Brooklyn Museum, New York, New York.*

69. Armchair, United States, 1850-1860; mahogany. *The Stowe-Day Foundation, Hartford, Connecticut.*

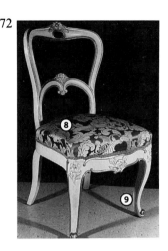

Curves in **C** or **S** shapes are the basis of furniture form. In the Rococo Revival Style, they mingle in decoration with scallop shells, leaves, flowers—especially the rose—baskets of flowers, the acanthus, and the cabochon. Legs are cabriole in form and often terminate in scroll feet. Contemporaries knew this style as the *Louis Quatorze,* the *Louis Quinze,* or the *Antique French.*

Rococo taste in the court of Louis XV was the main precedent. Craftsmen made some reproductions, but form and decoration also ranged from French furniture of the late seventeenth century to the mid-eighteenth. Motifs are combined and boldly reinterpreted from original delicacy. Side tables, sofas, chairs, and other eighteenth-century forms are extended with the "tête-à-tête," chairs with curved backs, and the étagère, or whatnot, for displaying objects.

Sources dictated walnut and painted woods. Rosewood and mahogany are common. Woods are laminated, as in the Naturalistic Style, for achieving delicate designs. Cast iron briefly appears in sophisticated furniture (No. 75).

The revival emerged in England and France during the 1820s, became a movement by the 1840s, and reigned in America during the 1850s. Designers often combined the cabriole leg and motifs with the Naturalistic Style. Features survived in mass-produced furniture into the 1880s.

1. Mirror
2. Rose flower and leaves
3. Cabriole leg
4. Acanthus leaf
5. Cartouche
6. **S** scroll
7. **C** scroll
8. Silk damask upholstery
9. Scroll foot
10. Finial
11. Console
12. Serpentine curve
13. Scallop shell
14. Marble top
15. Shell motif
16. Apron or skirt
17. Basket of flowers
18. Fruit motif
19. Carved hound chasing fox (opposite side)
20. Castor
21. Saltire stretcher

70. Étagère, New York City, 1850-1870; rosewood with laminated woods and marble top. *The Art Institute of Chicago, Elizabeth R. Vaughan Fund, Chicago, Illinois.*

71. Pier mirror, United States, circa 1853; gilt wood. *The Metropolitan Museum of Art, gift of Mrs. Frederick Wildman, 1964, New York, New York.*

72. Side chair, New York City, 1845-1855; painted and gilt mahogany. *The New York State Museum, Albany, New York.*

73. Étagère, New York City, 1850-1860; rosewood with marble top. *The Newark Museum, Newark, New Jersey, gift of the Museum of the City of New York.*

74. Center table, Doe, Hazelton and Company (label), Boston, Massachusetts, 1847-1857; mahogany and marble. *The Art Institute of Chicago, gift of Brooks and Hope B. McCormick, Chicago, Illinois.*

75. Center table, Walter Bryent designer for Chase Brothers and Company (label), Boston, Massachusetts, 1852; cast iron painted to simulate rosewood. *The Art Institute of Chicago, Wesley M. Dixon, Jr., Fund, Chicago, Illinois.*

76. Library table, John Henry Belter Firm (label), 1851-1861; rosewood. *The Art Institute of Chicago, gift of Gloria and Richard Manney, Chicago, Illinois.*

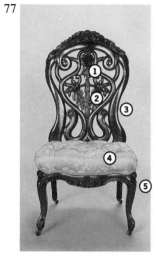

77

78

79

80

Fruit and flowers as well as leaves of the grape, oak, or rose are prominent in the Naturalistic Style. Carving is realistic, in contrast to generalization in the eighteenth century.

The style frequently merges with the contemporary Rococo Revival Style. Forms are identical and scrolls in *C* and *S* shapes, scallop shells, and the cabochon mingle with the motifs from nature.

Designs often are accomplished with a lamination process. Several layers of wood, each one-sixteenth of an inch thick, are glued together with the grain at right angles. Layers vary from three to sixteen, the average being six to eight. Panels are steamed in molds for undulating forms of such strength that a tracery of motifs could be carved into the backs of sofas and chairs or the skirts of tables. Superimposed carved elements increase the three-dimensional effect. Mahogany, walnut, and rosewood are favored as surface woods.

The style evolved with the English Rococo Revival during the 1820s. It assumed an original character in the United States through intricate carving integrated with form.

1. **Grapes and grape leaves**
2. **Oak leaves with acorns**
3. **Serpentine curve in laminated rosewood**
4. **Silk damask upholstery**
5. **Rose flowers and leaves**
6. **Marble top**
7. **Cabriole leg**
8. **Basket of flowers**
9. **Saltire stretcher**
10. **C scroll**
11. **S scroll**
12. **Putti (head of winged child)**
13. **Castor**

77. Side chair, John Henry Belter Firm (attributed), New York City, 1850-1867; laminated rosewood. *The Art Institute of Chicago, gift of Gloria and Richard Manney, Chicago, Illinois.*

78. Center table, John Henry Belter Firm (label), New York City, 1856-1861; rosewood with laminated woods and marble top. *The Museum of the City of New York, gift of Mr. and Mrs. Gunther Vieter, New York, New York.*

79. Bedstead, John Henry Belter Firm (label), New York City, 1850-1860; laminated rosewood. *The Brooklyn Museum, gift of Mrs. Ernest Vietor, New York, New York.*

80. Sofa, John and Joseph W. Meeks Firm (attributed), New York City, 1850-1860; laminated rosewood. *The Art Institute of Chicago, gift of Mrs. Anne McCall Dommerich, Mrs. Margaret McCall Dommerich, Mrs. Esther Foote, and Mrs. Charlotte McCall Ladd, in memory of Mr. and Mrs. Sumner T. McCall, Chicago, Illinois.*

81

82

83

84

85

Rectanglular shapes are contrasted with ovals and arches, straight and tapered legs are fluted, and plain surfaces are accented with classical moldings, columns, wreaths, garlands, urns, lyres, acanthus, and beading. The Louis XVI Style is the only revival in the mid-nineteenth century of an earlier period in form as well as decoration. But the revival is identified by bolder design and differences in craftsmanship and woods.

The long period of popularity includes many variations. They range from an initial period of exaggerated motifs in the 1850s and their close imitation in the 1860s to novel adaptations through the period.

Costly materials and elaborate workmanship are characteristic. Rosewood or ebonized woods are favored in the earliest versions. Walnut occurs with the 1890s. Dark woods contrast with gilt metal mounts, elaborate marquetry, panels of light woods, ivory inlays, and porcelain plaques. Carving is featured during the 1850s.

The English and the French originated this style. Eugenie, consort to Napoleon III, endorsed and popularized it after 1853, when it became known by the alternate name of the "Marie Antoinette" Style. The straight leg and motifs often are adapted to forms of the Renaissance Revival and Neo-Greek styles.

1. **Ormolu**
2. **Silk damask upholstery**
3. **Castor**
4. **Hinged top**
5. **Floral and ribbon carving**
6. **Tapered and fluted leg**
7. **Classical egg-and-dart motif**
8. **Ebonized maple**
9. **Ceramic plaque with ormolu frame**
10. **Incised gilt decoration**
11. **Marquetry**
12. **Porcelan plaque with ormolu frame**
13. **Amboina veneer**
14. **Ivory inlay**
15. **Ionic column with ormolu**
16. **Medial stretcher with urn**

81. Armchair, Leon Marcotte (attributed), New York City, 1856-1865; ebonized cherry and gilt metal mounts. *The Art Institute of Chicago, restricted gift of Marilyn and Thomas L. Karsten in honor of her parents, Gertrude and Perry S. Herst, Chicago, Illinois.*

82. Card table, Alexander Roux, New York City, 1850-1857; rosewood. *The Brooklyn Museum, H. Randolph Lever Fund, New York, New York.*

83. Cabinet (one of a pair), Leon Marcotte, New York City, circa 1860; ebonized maple with ormolu, ceramic plaque, and gilt moldings. *The Metropolitan Museum of Art, gift of Mrs. Chester D. Noyes, 1968, New York, New York.*

84. Cabinet, Alexander Roux, New York City, 1866; rosewood with porcelain plaques and gilt mounts. *The Metropolitan Museum of Art, Edgar J. Kaufmann, Jr., Charitable Foundation Fund, 1968, New York, New York.*

85. Library table, Leon Marcotte, New York City, 1862-1872; amboina with hornbeam, ivory inlay, and gilt metal mounts. *The Metropolitan Museum of Art, gift of Mrs. Robert W. de Forest, 1934, New York, New York.*

86

87

88

89

Renaissance Revival Style, 1850-1880

Renaissance, Baroque, and Mannerist approaches to design, especially in sixteenth- and seventeenth-century France, are combined in a period of vague historical knowledge to inspire the bold Renaissance Revival Style enduring through freedom of interpretation. Variations range from florid and curvilinear during the 1850s to severe and angular by the 1870s (see No. 103). Form enters the revival in the 1890s and survives to the 1920s. The Elizabethan Style is a variant based on English rather than French sources.

Common motifs are flowers, fruit, game, classical busts, bizarre faces known as "masks," acanthus scrolls, strapwork, and tassels. They are carved in high relief, and many recur in porcelain or marquetry insets on case furniture and table tops. Significant architectural motifs adapted to furniture are pediments, pilasters, columns, balusters, brackets, and volutes.

This style often merges in form and decoration with others. Cabriole legs and other elements of the Rococo Revival appear in the 1850s. They tend to disappear in the 1860s before straight legs and motifs from the Louis XVI Style or the cloven hoof associated with it and the Egyptian Revival.

Mahogany and walnut are favored woods. Rosewood and ebony are occasional. Burled walnut panels are featured by the 1870s. Upholstery, especially in chairs, is prominent.

1. Carved tassel
2. Classical woman's head (mask)
3. Louis XVI Revival leg
4. Castor
5. Grotesque mask
6. Acanthus scroll
7. Silk damask upholstery
8. Rococo Revival skirt and cabriole leg
9. Scroll foot
10. Console
11. Mirror
12. Baluster adaptation
13. Ball-foot adaptation
14. Finial
15. Strapwork adaptation
16. Carved floral bouquet in urn
17. Adaptation of cluster column

86. Armchair, John Jelliff, Newark, New Jersey, 1860-1870; rosewood. *The Newark Museum, gift of Mrs. John Laimbeer, Jr., Newark, New Jersey.*

87. Sofa, Charles A. Baudouine Firm (attributed), New York City, 1849-1854; laminated mahogany. *The Art Institute of Chicago, gift of Mr. and Mrs. Louis J. Fischer, Chicago, Illinois.*

88. Étagère, Julius Dessoir, New York City, 1855-1865; rosewood. *The Metropolitan Museum of Art, Edgar J. Kaufmann, Jr., Charitable Foundation Fund, 1969, New York, New York.*

89. Piano, Robert Nunns and John Clark, New York City, 1851; rosewood. *The Metropolitan Museum of Art, gift of George Lowther, 1906, New York, New York.*

90

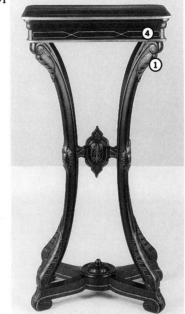

91

92

93

94

Curved and rectangular elements boldly contrast in shapes. Common motifs from ancient Greek architecture and ornament are pilasters, columns, flutes, acroteria, foliate scrolls, anthemia, and the Greek key design. They are carved in high relief, inlaid in contrasting light and dark woods, or incised and gilded.

The alternate names of "New" and "Modern" Greek identify a different interpretation of sources than in the earlier Classical Style. Motifs are exaggerated in size, changed in proportion, and combined in new ways. Taut curves and crisp angles are tensely balanced. The shapes of the Greek curule and *klismos* chairs are revived. Feet vary from the cloven hoof to scrolls. Case furniture often rests on a high plinth.

The French originated the Neo-Greek Style. It reached the United States in the late 1850s, became popular by the 1870s, and influenced factory furniture in the 1880s. Motifs often merge with the contemporary Louis XVI and Renaissance Revival styles.

1. **Anthemion**
2. **Greek curule shape**
3. **Hoof foot**
4. **Incised gilt lines**
5. **Boss**
6. **Fluted pilaster**
7. **Lion head**
8. **Medial stretcher**
9. **Castor**
10. **Finial**
11. **Burl walnut panel**
12. **Greek key design**
13. **Metal plaque**
14. **Plinth**

90. Stool, Alexander Roux, New York City, circa 1865; painted woods. *The Metropolitan Museum of Art, Edgar J. Kaufmann, Jr. Charitable Foundation Fund, 1969, New York, New York.*

91. Stand, New York City, circa 1870; ebonized cherry. *The Metropolitan Museum of Art, Edgar J. Kaufmann, Jr. Charitable Foundation Fund, 1969, New York, New York.*

92. Armchair, New York City, 1860-1870; ebonized wal- nut. *The Brooklyn Museum, gift of Sarah Fanning Chapman and Bertha Fanning Taylor, New York, New York.*

93. Bedstead, Nelson, Matter, and Company, Grand Rapids, Michigan, 1870-1880; walnut. *The Margaret Woodbury Strong Museum, gift of Mr. and Mrs. John C. Doolittle, Rochester, New York.*

94. Music cabinet, George Croome, Boston, Massachusetts, 1875-1877; mahogany, rosewood. *The Art Institute of Chicago, Elizabeth R. Vaughan Fund, Chicago, Illinois.*

95

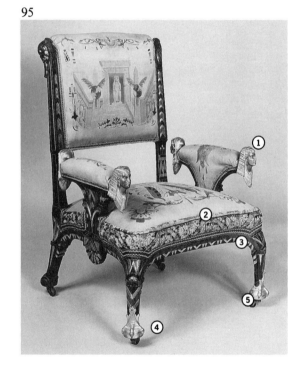

96

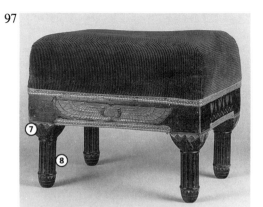

97

98

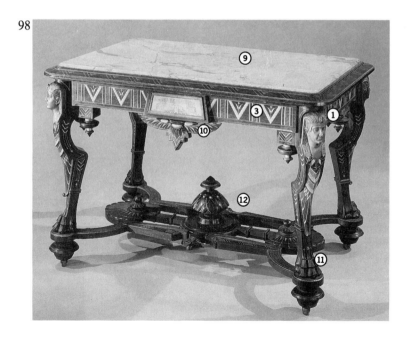

Egyptian heads, clustered columns, lotus capitals, winged orbs, zigzag lines, palmettes, the cloven hoof, and paw-shaped feet are Egyptian motifs emerging as occasional motifs early in the nineteenth century and combined with others late in the century for the Egyptian Revival Style. Popularity is limited.

Tables, chairs, stands, and stools mainly are common forms of the late nineteenth century with motifs adapted to them. The Egyptian stool with a concave seat and turned stretchers and legs is the principal revival of an ancient form.

Treatment of motifs may show contrasting elements, even on a single piece of furniture, from shallow relief to three-dimensional exuberance. Gilt decoration is common against dark and often ebonized woods. Exotic combinations of materials include woods, marble, and gilt bronze.

English fashion encouraged the Egyptian Style. Monuments or artifacts in tombs from about 2700 B.C. to about 1000 B.C. are the main source for motifs. Exhibition of Egyptian antiquities in the international exposition at London in 1862, completion of the Suez Canal in 1869, and British concern with Egyptian affairs after 1876 all stimulated interest in Egypt and Egyptian art.

1. **Bronze head**
2. **Tapestry upholstery**
3. **Gilt incised ornament**
4. **Claw-and-ball foot**
5. **Castor**
6. **Egyptian stool form**
7. **Lotus capital**
8. **Cluster column**
9. **Marble top**
10. **Winged orb**
11. **Lion-paw foot**
12. **Medial stretcher**

95. Armchair, New York City, 1870-1880; rosewood, gilt metal. *The Art Institute of Chicago, restricted gift of Suzanne Waller Worthy, Chicago, Illinois.*

96. Stool, United States, 1870-1880; oak. *The Newark Museum, bequest of Susan Dwight Bliss, Newark, New Jersey.*

97. Stool, United States, 1870-1880; maple painted black. *The Metropolitan Museum of Art, Rogers Fund, 1967, New York, New York.*

98. Center table, New York City, 1870-1880; rosewood, marble. *The Metropolitan Museum of Art, Edgar J. Kaufmann Jr. Charitable Foundation Fund, 1969, New York, New York.*

99

100

101

102

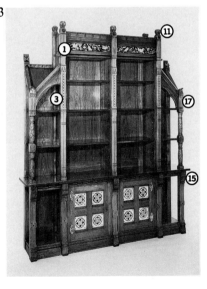

103

Reformed Gothic or Eastlake Style, 1870-1890

Charles Locke Eastlake was chagrined that Americans associated his name with shoddy, mass-produced furniture superficially inspired by simple English Medieval, Renaissance, and eighteenth-century furniture he endorsed for sound construction, practical form, and generalized decoration. Features of the true Reformed Gothic or Eastlake Style are rectangular forms in oak or cherry, with brackets, trestles, and decoration of grooves, chamfers, geometric ornament, and spindles. The style evolved during the 1870s and merges in factories with Neo-Greek and Renaissance Revival styles.

Eastlake became known through his *Hints on Household Taste,* published in London in 1868. Developed from magazine articles, the book reached nine American editions from 1872 to 1890. Eastlake endorses relationship between form, function, and craftsmanship, approves carving or inlay by hand, condemns machines for imitating handcraftsmanship and endorses machines for furniture meeting his standards.

Eastlake differed from William Morris and other English contemporaries concerned with reforming awkward shapes, abundant ornament, or careless craftsmanship. They often relied on medieval standards. Eastlake emphasized principles evident in many periods, including his own.

Art Furniture and Arts and Crafts furniture often suggest Eastlake's philosophy. Both include motifs reducing his concepts to a style.

1. **Incised lines**
2. **Chamfer**
3. **Geometric ornament**
4. **Ball foot**
5. **Crocket**
6. **Roman arch**
7. **Fielded panel**
8. **Spindles**
9. **Stylized leaves**
10. **Sunflowers and leaves**
11. **Finial**
12. **Cornice**
13. **Stylized flower**
14. **Triangle motif**
15. **Bracket**
16. **Grooves**
17. **Flying buttress (Gothic architectural adaptation)**

99. Pedestal, New York City, 1870-1880; ebonized cherry. *The Metropolitan Museum of Art, Edgar J. Kaufmann Jr. Charitable Foundation Fund, 1969, New York, New York.*

100. Sideboard, Herter Brothers (incised stamp), New York City, 1870-1876; oak, white pine. *The Art Institute of Chicago, Robert R. McCormick Charitable Trust, Chicago, Illinois.*

101. Armchair, New York City, circa 1876; maple. *Sagamore Hill, National Historic Site, Oyster Bay, New York.*

102. Bookcase, William Homes Company, Boston, Massachusetts, circa 1876; oak. *The Hudson River Museum, gift of the Doran Family, Yonkers, New York.*

103. Bookcase, Isaac E. Scott, Chicago, Illinois, 1875; walnut. *The Chicago Architecture Foundation, Chicago, Illinois.*

104

105

106

107

108

109

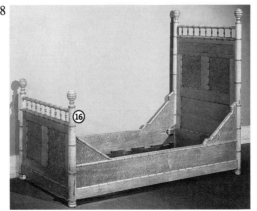

"Art" is vaguely linked to "Furniture" in an English trend toward new directions in design, craftsmanship, and ornament. Approaches vary from adaptations of the English Queen Anne mode of the 1880s to those published in London in 1877 in *Art Furniture Designed by Edward W. Godwin F.S.A. and Others, with Hints and Suggestions on Domestic Furniture and Decoration by William Watt.* The movement was popular into the 1890s and lingered to 1914.

Forms vary from simple to complex. Planes and angularity among some designers contrast with curves among others.

Ornament is diverse. It includes classical moldings, medieval spindles, and spiral turnings of the Restoration Style. Other sources range from oriental to Near Eastern, from Moorish to Egyptian. Japanese art received particular emphasis. It contributed the principle of asymmetrical composition, in such forms as cupboards or the arrangement of motifs, and encouraged stylized, two-dimensional designs. Decoration is achieved by shallow carving, marquetry, or inlaid woods and metals.

Woods vary. Some are stained black, to suggest ebony and lacquer. Bamboo is imported, and imitations in maple repeat a motif in the Windsor Style of the late eighteenth and early nineteenth centuries.

1. Finial
2. Face (dial and spandrels)
3. Brass inlay
4. Ebonized finish
5. Marquetry of cherry blossoms
6. Silk damask upholstery
7. Floral relief carving
8. Reeded leg
9. Glass-ball foot
10. Cornice
11. Putto head with wings
12. Carving background stippled and stained brown
13. Column fluting as a decorative band
14. Gilt hardware
15. Fielded panels
16. Bamboo turnings
17. Brass gallery in Near Eastern design
18. Japanese lacquer
19. Marquetry of rose motifs
20. Gilt lines
21. Carved flowers with gilt stamens
22. Egyptian revival paw feet
23. Display area

104. Clock, George Grant Elmslie and William Purcell, designers, Chicago, Illinois, for Niedecken Walbridge Company, 1912; mahogany with brass and wood inlays. From the Henry B. Babson House, Riverside, Illinois. *The Art Institute of Chicago, gift of Mrs. Theodore D. Tiecken, Chicago, Illinois.*

105. Side chair, Herter Brothers, New York City, 1876-1884; ebonized cherry. *The Art Institute of Chicago, Mrs. Alfred S. Burdick Fund, Chicago, Illinois.*

106. Armchair, Louis Comfort Tiffany and associates, New York City, 1890; unidentified wood. *The Shelburne Museum, Shelburne, Vermont.*

107. Chest of drawers, New York City, 1874-1884; maple with cherry. Commissioned by Henry G. Marquand (1819-1902). *The Art Institute of Chicago, gift of the Antiquarian Society through the Mr. and Mrs. William Y. Hutchinson Fund, Chicago, Illinois.*

108. Bedstead, probably New York City, 1875-1885; maple. *The Metropolitan Museum of Art, Edgar J. Kaufmann Jr. Charitable Foundation Fund, 1969, New York, New York.*

109. Sideboard, Herter Brothers (incised stamp), New York City, 1876-1884; rosewood with cherry, maple, walnut, and satinwood. *The Art Institute of Chicago, gift of the Antiquarian Society through the Capital Campaign Fund, Chicago, Illinois.*

110

111

112

113

Art Nouveau Style, 1896-1914

Sinuous curves often dominate form and decoration. Common motifs are naturalistic and stylized tulips, lilies, poppies, and leaves. The Art Nouveau Style in furniture held limited appeal, and few examples survive.

An exposition at Paris in 1900 popularized this style internationally. It had originated in Paris, with encouragement by the art dealer Siegfried Bing. He featured it in his shop, known as the Maison de l'Art Nouveau, from the opening late in 1895 until the closing early in 1904. Designers created for Bing's clients costly handmade interpretations of their "Modern Art," which was inspired particularly by the curving line in Japanese art and French eighteenth-century Rococo art.

Sophisticated American furniture reveals influence of the Art Nouveau Style, particularly in ornament, shortly before 1900 and until 1914. During this period, the style frequently influences curved lines in revival styles, and ornament occurs on mass-produced furniture as well as in the Arts and Crafts styles. There was a brief vogue for the style among furniture manufacturers from 1900 to about 1903.

1. **Glass door**
2. **Mirrored back panel**
3. **Relief-carved poppies**
4. **"Whiplash" curved lines**
5. **Gothic crocket as pendant**
6. **Medial and side stretcher**
7. **Form: Queen Ann Style revival**
8. **Relief-carved flower buds**
9. **Cabriole leg**

110. Cabinet, George C. Flint and Company, Chicago, Illinois, circa 1910; mahogany. *The Metropolitan Museum of Art, Edgar J. Kaufmann, Jr. Charitable Foundation Fund, 1968, New York, New York.*

111. Stand, United States, 1900-1915; mahogany. *The Margaret Woodbury Strong Museum, Rochester, New York.*

112. Side chair, Charles Rohlfs, designer, Buffalo, New York, circa 1898; oak. *The Art Museum, Princeton University, gift of Roland Rohlfs, Princeton, New Jersey.*

113. Corner chair, probably New York City, 1900-1915; mahogany. The Art Institute of Chicago, restricted gift of Dr. and Mrs. Edwin J. DeCosta, Chicago, Illinois.

114

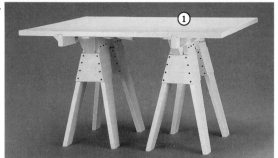

115

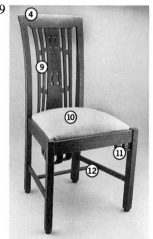

116

117

118

119

120

Handcraftsmanship, or its appearance, is a theme among individualistic approaches to furniture that are generally identified in America and with the Arts and Crafts movement. Furniture usually is rectilinear and often offers a relationship between form and function. Ornament among different designers is oriental, medieval, Renaissance, Gothic or Art Nouveau in inspiration.

The Arts and Crafts movement evolved from British opinion that machines were lowering standards of form, decoration, and craftsmanship. Various efforts combining reform of the arts with reform of industrial society reached America with diverse results. The principal themes are William Morris's emphasis on medieval art, E. W. Godwin's solutions in the Art Furniture movement, and Charles Locke Eastlake's principles.

Solutions are individual, but the movement is national. Innovative architects in Illinois, encouraged by Frank Lloyd Wright, and in California by Charles and Henry Greene, designed furniture sympathetic with their buildings. George Niedecken in the Midwest, Lucia K. Mathews and Arthur F. Mathews on the West Coast, and Elbert Hubbard, with the brothers Gustav, Leopold, and J. George Stickley on the East Coast are among the diverse contributors to the movement.

Oak is a common wood. The use of it is a revival of an English and American material from the Medieval and Renaissance styles.

1. **White enamel paint**
2. **Leather upholstery**
3. **Carved and painted panel drops for writing surface**
4. **Ebony pegs covering screws**
5. **Inlays of abalone shell, silver, and copper**
6. **Wooden drawer knobs**
7. **Relief carved tulip**
8. **Linenfold carving**
9. **Splat in Chinese taste**
10. **Slip seat**
11. **Bracket in Chinese taste**
12. **Medial and side stretchers**
13. **Pewter and copper inlays**

114. Breakfast table, Louis Comfort Tiffany, designer for Ernest Hagen and J. Matthew Meier workshop, New York City, 1885; pine painted white. From the Tiffany House, Madison Avenue at 72nd Street, New York City. *The Art Institute of Chicago, anonymous gift, Chicago, Illinois.*

115. Armchair, Louis Comfort Tiffany, designer for Ernest Hagen and J. Matthew Meier workshop, New York City, 1885; maple painted white with brown leather upholstery. From the Tiffany House, Madison Avenue at 72nd Street, New York City. *The Art Institute of Chicago, anonymous gift, Chicago, Illinois.*

116. Desk, Lucia K. Mathews and Arthur F. Mathews, San Francisco, California, 1906-1918; walnut. *The Oakland Museum Association, gift of the Art Guild, Oakland, California.*

117. Serving table, Charles Sumner Greene designer for Peter and John Hall workshop, Pasadena, California, 1907-1909; mahogany with ebony pegs and inlays of silver, copper, and abalone. From the Robert R. Blacker House, Pasadena, California. *The Art Institute of Chicago, Wentworth Greene Field Memorial Fund and Maurice D. Galleher Fund, Chicago, Illinois.*

118. Library table, design by George Washington Maher Firm, Chicago, Illinois, 1905; oak. From the Emil Rudolph House, Highland Park, Illinois. *The Art Institute of Chicago, Robert R. McCormick Charitable Trust Fund, Chicago, Illinois.*

119. Side chair, Charles Sumner Greene designer for Peter and John Hall workshop, Pasadena, California, 1907-1909; mahogany with ebony pegs. From the Robert R. Blacker House, Pasadena, California. *The Art Institute of Chicago, restricted gift of the Graham Foundation, Chicago, Illinois.*

120. Rocking chair, Harvey Ellis, designer for Gustav Stickley workshop, Eastwood, New York, 1903; oak with pewter and copper inlays and leather upholstery. *The Art Institute of Chicago, gift of Mrs. Sidney Haskins, Chicago, Illinois.*

121

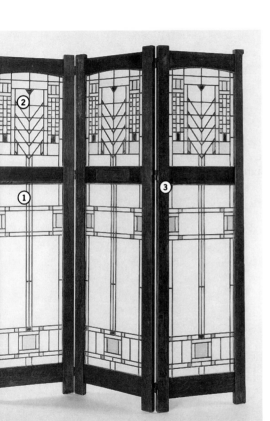

122

123

124

125

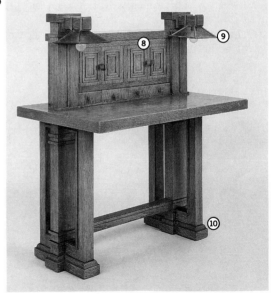

Prairie School Style, 1900-1920

Furniture combines international innovative concepts with architectural concerns of Frank Lloyd Wright and his disciples in the Midwestern Prairie School. Stained or fumed oak is the favored wood. Craftsmanship varies from crude to sophisticated.

Basic themes in Wright's architecture recur in the furniture. Forms are rectilinear, include cantilevered elements, and stress horizontal lines. Surfaces are mostly unadorned. When ornament occurs, it is geometric and stylized. Wright and others encouraged use of machines in preparing materials and developing ornament.

Prairie School architects designed furniture for overall harmony between a building and its furnishings. But without evidence furniture designs cannot be attributed to an architect responsible for a building. Wright's firm, for example, designed some furniture, but his reliance on staff or craftsmen for designing other furniture is unknown. Equally uncertain is his participation in designs by the firm of George M. Niedecken and John S. Walbridge that received Wright's commissions for several interiors. Niedecken, the partner active as a designer, had been closely associated with Wright and understood his concepts. Even he worked independently on some projects: he included classical moldings on a desk designed for Wright's Coonley House during a period in which Wright had abandoned such details (No. 125).

Many sources abroad inspired design elements in furniture associated with the Prairie School. The English Arts and Crafts Movement is the general background. Specific features of various forms originate in the contemporary European centers of innovative design. They range from tall backs on chairs, for example, in the designs of Charles Rennie Mackintosh of Scotland to the affinity of modular decoration in Purcell, Elmslie, and Fieck's chair to one by Koloman Moser of Austria (No. 123). The means of transmission often are difficult to trace in an era of convenient travel, photographs, and publications.

1. **Caming**
2. **Colored and clear glass**
3. **Hinges**
4. **Leather upholstery**
5. **Blocks as design elements**
6. **Seat cantilever**
7. **Ball foot**
8. **Applied bands**
9. **Glass shades over electric light bulbs**
10. **Ogee, or cyma recta, molding**

121. Screen, frame by George M. Niedecken (label), glass production by Linden Glass Company, glass design by Frank Lloyd Wright; Milwaukee, Wisconsin, and Chicago, Illinois, 1902-1907; oak and glass. Frame includes bronze plaque which states: "The Art and Craft of the Machine/A Lecture by Frank Lloyd Wright/Hull House March 6, 1901/Chicago Arts and Crafts Society." *The Art Institute of Chicago, gift of Mr. and Mrs. F. M. Fahernwald, by exchange, Chicago, Illinois.*

122. Side chair, Frank Lloyd Wright Firm, Chicago, Illinois, 1904; oak with leather upholstery. From the Larkin Building, Buffalo, New York. *The Art Institute of Chicago, Bessie Bennett Fund, Chicago, Illinois.*

123. Armchair, William Gray Purcell, George Feick, and George Grant Elmslie Firm, Milwaukee, Wisconsin, 1911-1912; oak with leather upholstery. From the Merchants Bank, Winona, Minnesota. *The Art Institute of Chicago, Fern and Manfred Steinfeld Fund, Chicago, Illinois.*

124. Side chair, George Grant Elmslie, designer, Chicago, Illinois, circa 1910; oak. Original location unknown. *The Art Institute of Chicago, gift of the Antiquarian Society through Mrs. William P. Boggess II, Chicago, Illinois.*

125. Desk, Niedecken Walbridge Company, Milwaukee, Wisconsin, circa 1910; oak. From the Avery Coonley House, Riverside, Illinois. *The Art Institute of Chicago, gift of The Graham Foundation for Advanced Studies in the Fine Arts, Chicago, Illinois.*

126

①

127

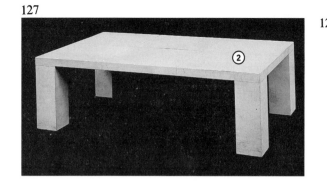

②

128

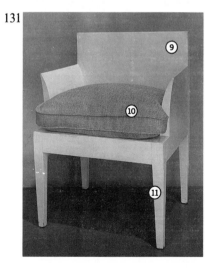

③ ④

129

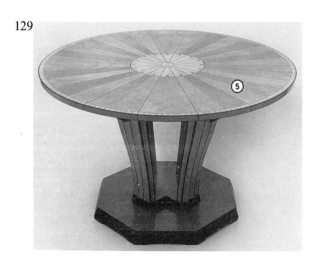

⑤

130

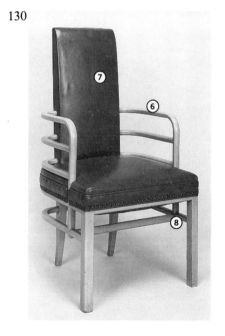

⑦ ⑥ ⑧

131

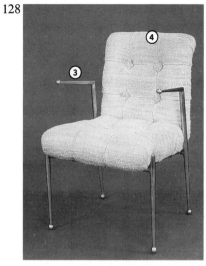

⑨ ⑩ ⑪

Art Deco Styles, 1925-1945

Controlled curves or crisp angles, monumental or delicate forms, and traditional wood or innovative steel are features of the greatly varying Art Deco movement in design. Common themes among the variations are simplicity of shape, emphasis on planes, and smooth surfaces.

Known to contemporaries as "Modern," the styles of the period are broadly identified today as "Art Deco." The term is derived from the Parisian event of 1925 that popularized the shift in taste and was titled "l'Exposition Internationale des Arts Décorative et Industriels Modernes."

The immediate result of the exposition was a style of attenuated forms, lavish veneers, and boldly contrasting inlays in the tradition that Eliel Saarinen commanded. Americans were equally open to other influences. Design gradually shifted in quality furniture of the 1930s to clarity of form as differently expressed as in the designs of Donald Deskey or Samuel Marx. Use of metal and experiments with construction reveal influences from the contemporary International Style abroad.

Fine craftsmanship and lavish materials are features of quality furniture. Surfaces vary from veneers and inlays of unusual woods to lacquer, parchment, and glass. The cocktail table is an innovation, chair backs are low and high, and upholstery varies from restrained to opulent.

1. **Wool upholstery**
2. **White leather surface**
3. **Steel**
4. **White wool upholstery**
5. **Harewood veneer with ebony, box, holly inlays**
6. **Green shellac**
7. **Red leather upholstery**
8. **Medial and side stretcher**
9. **White parchment surface**
10. **Wool cushion**
11. **Federal Style tapered leg**

126. Armchair, Donald Deskey, designer, New York City, 1932; mahogany with leather upholstery. *Radio City Music Hall, New York, New York.*

127. Cocktail table, Sameul Marx, designer for the William Quigley Company, Chicago, Illinois, 1944; white leather over wood. From the Leigh B. Block apartment, Chicago, Illinois. *The Art Institute of Chicago, gift of Leigh B. Block, Chicago, Illinois.*

128. Armchair, Donald Deskey, designer for the Royal Chrome Company, New York City, circa 1938; steel, with wool upholstery, by Dorothy Liebes. From the Samuel Marx apartment, Chicago, Illinois. *The Art Institute of Chicago, gift of Mrs. Florene Schoenborn, Chicago, Illinois.*

129. Dining table, Eliel Saarinen, designer for the Company of Master Craftsmen, Bloomfield Hills, Michigan, 1930; hare, ebony, box, and holly woods. *The Cranbrook Academy of Art and Museum, Bloomfield Hills, Michigan.*

130. Armchair, Kem Weber, designer for the Grand Rapids Chair Company, Grand Rapids, Michigan, 1928-1929; unidentified woods with green shellac and red leather upholstery. *The Art Institute of Chicago, Fern and Manfred Steinfeld Fund, Chicago, Illinois.*

131. Armchair, Hammond Kroll, designer, New York City, circa 1935; parchment over wood, with wool cushion, by Helen Kroll Kramer. *The Smithsonian Institution, The Cooper-Hewitt Museum of Design, gift of Helen Kroll Kramer in memory of Dr. Milton Lurie, New York, New York.*

132

133

134

①

②

135

①

136

④

③

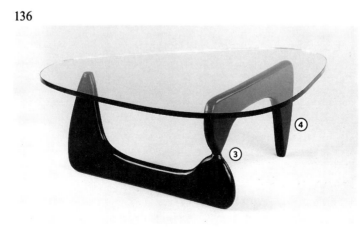

137

⑤

⑥

Industrial materials and industrial production meet objectives of furniture independent of traditional styles. The concept originated in continental Europe after World War I.

The Bauhaus, a school founded in Germany at Weimar and later moved to Dessau and Berlin, became the center of the new movement in the 1920s through Walter Gropius, Ludwig Miës van der Rohe, and Marcel Breuer. These leaders of the Bauhaus and other immigrants in the 1930s established the approach in American design.

The Museum of Modern Art encouraged the movement in 1940 with a competition for domestic furnishings. Eero Saarinen and Charles Eames won first prizes for a chair design and standardized tables and case furniture. The revolutionary chair combined seat, back, and arms into one unit of laminated woods formed in a mold. The design potential was realized after World War II, when Saarinen and Eames became innovators in the movement for industrially produced furniture in plastic, plywood, and metal.

Breuer's intent and that of other Europeans in the 1920s and 1930s was furniture without "style". But furniture designed in the International Style clearly reveals different aesthetic preferences among designers, as well as the influence of other contemporary movements in the arts.

1. **Molded laminated woods**
2. **Medial and side stretchers**
3. **Base pivot**
4. **Black shellac**
5. **Molded plastic**
6. **Aluminum**

132. Armchair, Harry Bertoia, designer for Knoll International, East Greenville, Pennsylvania, 1956; steel with vinyl upholstery. *The Art Institute of Chicago, gift of Malcolm, Kay, Kim, and Kyle Kamin, Chicago, Illinois.*

133. Coffee table, George Nelson, designer for Herman Miller Company, Zeeland, Michigan, 1963; chrome and glass. *The Art Institute of Chicago, gift of Malcolm, Kay, Kim, and Kyle Kamin, Chicago, Illinois.*

134. Side chair, Eero Saarinen and Larry Perkins, designers for the Illinois WPA Craft Project, Chicago, Illinois, 1940; birch and laminated birch. *The Art Institute of Chicago, gift of the Crow Island School, Chicago, Illinois.*

135. Side chair, Charles Eames, designer for Evans Products Company, Plymouth, Michigan, 1947-1949: laminated woods. *The Art Institute of Chicago, gift of Mrs. Eugene A. Davidson, Chicago, Illinois.*

136. Coffee table, Isamu Noguchi, designer for Herman Miller Company, Zeeland, Michigan, 1944; birch and glass. *The Art Institute of Chicago, gift of Malcom, Kay, Kim, and Kyle Kamin, Chicago, Illinois.*

137. Armchair, Eero Saarinen, designer for Knoll International, East Greenville, Pennsylvania, 1956; plastic, aluminum. *The Art Institute of Chicago, gift of Knoll International, Chicago, Illinois.*

138

139

140

141

142

143

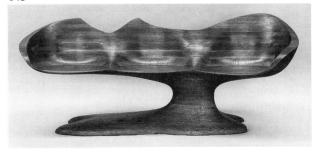

Execution varies from a craftsman personally creating unique furniture to his supervising others in making his designs. Iron or plastics are occasional materials, but the general concern is with traditional wood.

The movement has evolved nationally since the late 1940s. It is a reaction to standardized industrial furniture, and it continues the philosophy of personal expression from the Arts and Crafts period. Wharton Esherick is a link to craftsmen and their ideals at the turn of the twentieth century through his example from the 1920s to the 1960s.

Personal styles reflect greatly varying intellectual and emotional responses to furniture as a practical, sculptural, or even a humorous element in daily life. Forms may be rectilinear, abstract, or occasionally anthropomorphic and biomorphic. Some designers and craftsmen have turned to historic styles for inspiration.

Woods may be selected for uniformity of color and grain, chosen for irregularities, or laminated for the potential of form, strength, and decoration. Production is equally diverse. It may rely on hand craftsmanship or modern technology in any phase of preparing, forming, and finishing woods.

138. Table entitled *Demi-Lune Table,* Wendell Castle, designer and John Zanetti, craftsman, Scottsville, New York, 1985; rosewood with ziricote veneer on top and ivory for inlay and feet. *The Art Institute of Chicago, Raymond W. Garbe Fund in honor of Carl A. Erickson, Sr., Chicago, Illinois.*

139. Looking glass, Daniel K. Jackson, Philadelphia, Pennsylvania, 1973; rosewood, Osage orange. *The Philadelphia Museum of Art, gift of the Friends of the Philadelphia Museum of Art, Philadelphia, Pennsylvania.*

140. Double music rack, Wharton Esherick, Paoli, Pennsylvania, 1962; walnut, cherry. *The Wharton Esherick Museum, Paoli, Pennsylvania.*

141. Cradle-cabinet, Sam Maloof, Alta Loma, California, 1968; laminated walnut. *American Craft Museum, gift of the Johnson Wax Company, New York, New York.*

142. Chest-table, Wharton Esherick, Paoli, Pennsylvania, 1969; walnut. *The American Craft Museum, gift of the Johnson Wax Company, New York, New York.*

143. Sofa, Wendell Castle, Scottsville, New York, 1967; laminated oak. From the Lee Nordness apartment, New York City. *The Art Institute of Chicago, gift of Karen Johnson Boyd, Chicago, Illinois.*

144

145

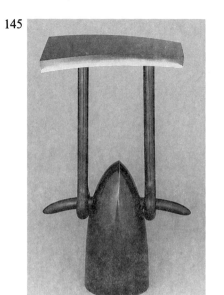

146

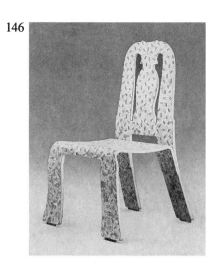

147

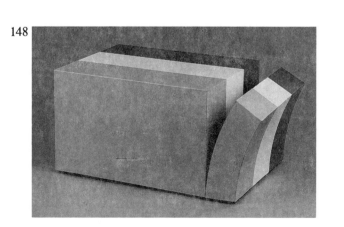

148

149

Contemporary Styles, 1981-Present

Challenges to the International Style prevailing since the 1950s gradually gained a public through the influence of Italian design in the 1970s. The rebellion crystallized in 1981 with designs by an Italian colllaboration known as Memphis. Named for the city in the United States, it included such Americans as Peter Shire. Restless attitudes in the United States toward intellectualized and impersonal furniture is evidenced in mass-produced industrial furniture as well as handcrafted unique objects.

Approaches greatly differ among designers, but their basic theme is reversing principles of the International Style. Function does not determine form. Colors are the rule, not the exception, and unusual combinations are typical. Surface patterns are embraced, not omitted. History is teased, instead of revered, as in Venturi's version of a chair in the Queen Anne Style (No. 146).

Popular culture is one source of the new aesthetic. Pop Art became a theme in American painting and sculpture during the early 1960s but was dormant by the 1970s. Lee Payne's *Neapolitan Table* forcefully represents the recurrence of the theme in the 1980s through the reference to a block of chocolate, vanilla, and strawberry ice cream (No. 148).

Many objects offer whimsical and erratic elements. Lewis & Clark envision the god-like occupant of their *Temple Chair* activating unseen ceremonies of an imaginary cult (No. 147). The *Phidias Chair* is Peter Shire's essay in geometric forms dramatized by the impression of precarious balance (No. 149). Wendell Castle's giant hooks support the top of *Lucky Table* that is carved to seem warped and impractical (No. 145).

Emotional response is the innovative designer's objective. Changes in the usual form, scale, color, texture, surface pattern or concept often are meant to shock the viewer into a new awareness. His environment then can become one in which furniture is art and art is furniture.

144. *Easy Chair,* Forrest Myers, designer, New York City, 1983; anodized steel. *The Art Institute of Chicago, Raymond W. Garbe Fund in honor of Carl A. Erickson, Sr., Chicago, Illinois.*

145. *Lucky Table,* Wendell Castle, designer and craftsman, Scottsville, New York, 1986; stained and painted cherry and curly maple veneer. *The Art Institute of Chicago, Raymond W. Garbe Fund in honor of Carl A. Erickson, Sr., Chicago, Illinois.*

146. Side chair, Robert Venturi, designer, for Knoll International, 1984; laminated plywood and plastic. *The Art Institute of Chicago, gift of Mr. Marshall Cogan and Knoll International Holdings, Inc., Chicago, Illinois. (Photograph: Courtesy of Knoll International.)*

147. *Temple Chair,* Lewis & Clark (James Angivine Lewis and Clark Edward Ellefson), Columbia, South Carolina, 1983; Colorcore Formica on various woods. *The Art Institute of Chicago, gift of the Formica Corporation, Chicago, Illinois.*

148. *Neopolitan Table,* Lee Payne, Atlanta, Georgia, 1983; Colorcore Formica on various woods. *The Art Institute of Chicago, gift of Lee Payne, Chicago, Illinois.*

149. *Phidias Chair,* Peter Shire, designer, Los Angeles, California, 1984; baked enamel on steel. *The Oakland Museum, Rena Bransten Fund, Oakland, California.*

150

151

152

153

154

Dutch Style, 1624-1860

Seventeenth-century immigrants to Dutch claims in the mid-Atlantic region introduced furniture designs continuing in isolated areas in northern New Jersey, on Long Island, and in the Hudson River Valley long after the major settlement of New Amsterdam became the prominent English community of New York City. Diverse origins of the colonists in the Netherlands and their equally diverse sophistication are evident in the recorded furniture.

The practical *kas,* common in northern Europe during the seventeenth century for storing clothing, linens, and other personal articles, is a major form. It survives in many variations. They range from seventeenth-century versions in oak and eighteenth-century examples in walnut, maple, or tulip with painted decoration, to early nineteenth-century mahogany examples with inlays in the Federal Style.

Other furniture forms and their decoration reveal continental influences. Turnings are elaborate on chairs and tables. Curves are complex on cupboards or other forms, such as the multipurpose chair-table with a storage compartment beneath the chair seat and a back lowering to become a table top. Simple tables include stretchers between legs as well as central diagonal braces between top and base.

1. **Ovolo molding with raised panels**
2. **Fielded panels**
3. **Boss**
4. **Drawer**
5. **Ball foot**
6. **Finial**
7. **Blue-green paint**
8. **Flat arm rest**
9. **Turned support**
10. **Rush seat**
11. **Cornice**
12. **Black, gray, white decoration**
13. **Back tilts for table**
14. **Seat lifts for storage**
15. **Medial stretcher**
16. **Trestle base**
17. **Cross stretchers**
18. **Chamfered corner**

150. *Kas* (wardrobe), New York City area, 1650-1700; oak. *The Art Institute of Chicago, Sanford Fund, Chicago, Illinois.*

151. Armchair, Kings County, Queens County, or New York City, 1680-1700; oak painted blue-green. *The Art Institute of Chicago, Sewell L. Avery Fund, Chicago, Illinois.*

152. *Kas* (wardrobe), New York City area, 1700-1735; tulip with black, gray, white painted decoration. *The*

Henry Francis du Pont Winterthur Museum, Winterthur, Delaware.

153. Chair-table, Hudson River Valley, 1690-1740; maple oak. *The Art Institute of Chicago, gift of Jamee J. and Marshall Field, in honor of Nancy J. and Milo M. Naeve, Chicago, Illinois.*

154. Table, Hudson River Valley, 1725-1775; maple and tulip painted gray. *Historic Hudson Valley, Van Cortlandt Manor House, Tarrytown, New York.*

55

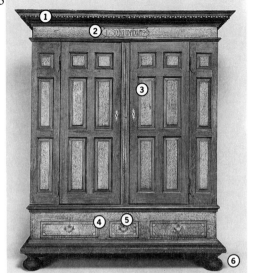

156

157

58

159

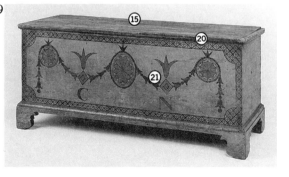

German Style, 1750-1870

Germanic immigrants from central Europe to New York, North Carolina, and southeastern Pennsylvania introduced a style flourishing by the late eighteenth century. Immigration to Virginia and Ohio from earlier settlements and abroad introduced Germanic culture to other regions. The Germans initially continued seventeenth- and eighteenth-century forms abroad for chairs, chests, tables, and other furniture. American variations of Germanic decorations soon were adapted to traditional chests, boxes, and wardrobes known as *shonks,* as well as to such English forms as chests of drawers, clocks, and desks with bookcases. The German Style flourished through the early nineteenth century. It lost vigor at mid-century with the dissipation of German culture and access to mass-produced furniture.

Storage chests of tulip wood for men and women are the favored form. Elaborate versions are brightly painted in red, blue, white, and yellow, with tulips, hearts, birds, stars, and unicorns. Walnut inlaid with white sulphur designs of scrolls, pilasters, hearts, and shells are a distinctive and smaller group. Names and initials of owners and commemorative dates frequently document pride of possession.

1. **Cornice with dentil variation**
2. **Owner name and date: "17 John Weidner 90"**
3. **Blue-green, coral, and white paint**
4. **Drawer**
5. **Painted version of Federal Style inlay**
6. **Ball foot**
7. **Hand grip**
8. **Legs extend through seat**
9. **Cleats support legs**
10. **Form adapts Philadelphia Chippendale Style**
11. **Finial**
12. **Blue-green and white paint**
13. **Loper**
14. **Ogee bracket foot**
15. **Hinged top with battens**
16. **Sulphur inlay in walnut**
17. **Pilaster**
18. **Foliate scrolls**
19. **Fluting (inlaid representation)**
20. **Green, red, and black paint**
21. **Germanic tulips with Neoclassic paterae, swags, and bellflowers**

155. *Shonk* (wardrobe), Oley area, Pennsylvania, 1790; tulip with blue, white, red painted decoration. *The Art Institute of Chicago, Elizabeth R. Vaughan Fund, Chicago, Illinois.*

156. Side chair, Zoar, Ohio, circa 1817-1837; chestnut and oak. *The Art Institute of Chicago, restricted gift of Jamee J. and Marshall Field and Mr. and Mrs. John Trumbull; Sewell L. Avery and Elizabeth Vaughan Funds; and Charles F. Montgomery and Charlotte Olson, by exchange, Chicago, Illinois.*

157. Desk and bookcase, eastern Pennsylvania, 1780-1810; pine, painted blue-green and white. *The Henry Francis du Pont Winterthur Museum, Winterthur, Delaware.*

158. Chest, Ephrata area, Pennsylvania, 1783; walnut with sulphur inlay. *The Smithsonian Institution, Washington, D.C.*

159. Chest, Albany or Schoharie Counties, New York, 1807-1816; white pine. *Gift of the Antiquarian Society through the Juli and David Grainger Fund, Chicago, Illinois.*

160

161

163

162

165

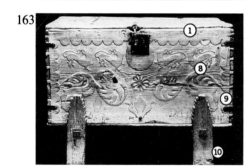

164

Spanish Style, 1600-1900

Furniture was rare in Spanish territories across the present southern United States. Surviving examples are mainly from New Mexico, where scarce tools, hinges and locks were imported about 2,000 miles overland from Mexico City.

Life in Santa Fe, founded in 1610, was simple. Beyond the capital, it was primitive. Until the nineteenth century, tables, chairs, benches, and beds were unknown except for those in churches or prosperous households. The earliest survivals are from the eighteenth century and continue traditions for simple furniture in seventeenth- and eighteenth-century Spain.

Chests are the common form. They rest on the floor, on stands, or on legs. The other traditional forms are *alacenas* (wall cupboards), *repisos* (shelves), *tarmitas* (stools), and *trasteros* (cupboards).

Decoration is simple. Chests, cupboards, and shelves include geometric designs or generalized motifs, such as flowers, shells, rosettes, scrolls, and occasionally animals. Motifs are carved in relief or painted in yellow, red, blue, black, and white. Grooves and chip carving are common.

Soft Ponderosa pine is the principal wood. The difficulty of preparing it, before the introduction of sawmills in 1846, resulted in reworking parts from worn or damaged furniture.

1. Hinged top
2. Triangle motif
3. Fielded panel with relief carving
4. Channel molding
5. Exposed mortise-and-tenon joint
6. Spindles
7. Hinged door with spindles
8. Relief-carved lions, rabbits, foliate scrolls
9. Exposed dovetail joint
10. Separate stand
11. Indian stepped design symbolizes heaven and rain
12. Relief-carved panels of lions, rosettes, pomegranates
13. Batten

160. Chest, possibly by Francisco A. Valdez, Taos-Santa Cruz Area, New Mexico, circa 1812; Ponderosa pine. From the Ranchos de Taos Church. *The Art Institute of Chicago, restricted gift of Warren L. Batts, Wesley M. Dixon, Jr., Jamee J. and Marshall Field, Mrs. Frank L. Sulzberger, and an anonymous donor in honor of Nelson E. Smyth, Chicago, Illinois.*

161. Armchair, northern New Mexico, 1775-1800; Ponderosa pine. *Museum of New Mexico, Santa Fe, New Mexico. (Negative No. 25647.)*

162. Food cupboard, northern New Mexico, 1800-1850; Ponderosa pine. *The American Museum in Britain, Claverton Manor, Bath, England.*

163. Chest with stand, northern New Mexico, 1780-1800; Ponderosa pine. *Museum of New Mexico, Santa Fe, New Mexico. (Negative No. 65701.)*

164. Arm chair, Santa Fe area, New Mexico, 1776-1821; Ponderosa pine. *The Art Institute of Chicago, restricted gift of Mr. and Mrs. Robert A. Kubicek, Chicago, Illinois.*

165. Chest, northern New Mexico, 1780-1820; Ponderosa pine. *The American Museum in Britain, Claverton Manor, Bath, England.*

166

167

168

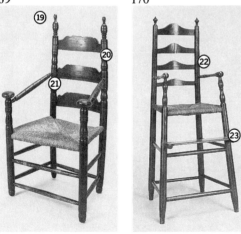

169

170

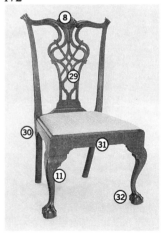

171

172

Furniture in many traditions includes six-board chests and trestle tables of the Medieval Style, joined and turned forms, modifications of sophisticated styles, or is new in concept. Spanish, Dutch, and German emigrants evolved other traditions, forming distinct styles.

Significant among designs original to America are late seventeenth-century dower chests, carved in low relief with tulips, hearts, and other motifs popular in the isolated Connecticut River Valley. They are known as "Hadley" chests—after the town of Hadley, Massachusetts—but craftsmen made them over several generations from Hartford, Connecticut, to Deerfield, Massachusetts (No. 166).

Tables occur in many variations. One is known today as the "butterfly" type for the shape of the leaf supports (No. 168).

Common chairs follow a European tradition of shaped slats and turned legs introduced in America during the seventeenth century. The many variations range from high backs in New England—influenced by chairs of the William and Mary Style—to walnut chairs delicate in appearance, yet sturdy in construction, from Pennnsylvania.

Adaptations of sophisticated furniture may be contemporary with a style or may combine motifs from earlier styles. Furniture may be decorated with simple carving and painted.

Woods usually are local. Birch and maple often are stained imitations of mahogany.

1. **Hinged top with battens**
2. **Relief-carved tulips, leaves, hearts**
3. **Side rail**
4. **Rail**
5. **Stile**
6. **Knob handle**
7. **Cornice**
8. **Scallop shell**
9. **Ogee molding**
10. **S scroll**
11. **Cabriole leg**
12. **Square pad foot**
13. **Hinged leaf**
14. **"Butterfly" leaf support**
15. **Splay leg**
16. **Double baluster turning**
17. **Stretcher**
18. **Worn ball foot**
19. **Finial**
20. **Turned posts**
21. **Cyma curve**
22. **Concave arm for tying child**
23. **Footrest**
24. **Crest rail with yoke**
25. **Concave, urn-shaped splat**
26. **Side, medial, and back stretchers**
27. **Leaf-carving at knee**
28. **Trifid foot with raised panels**
29. **Chinese fret**
30. **Side rail**
31. **Front rail**
32. **Claw-and-ball foot**

166. Chest ("Hadley" type), Connecticut River Valley, 1670-1720; oak, white pine. *The Art Institute of Chicago, gift of the Robert R. McCormick Charitable Trust, Chicago, Illinois.*

167. Chest-on-chest, on frame, possibly by Samuel Dunlap, New Hampshire, 1780-1820; maple. *The Currier Gallery of Art, Manchester, New Hampshire.*

168. Table ("butterfly" type), Connecticut or western Massachusetts, 1710-1740; cherry and maple, painted red. *Historic Deerfield, Inc., Deerfield, Massachusetts.*

169. Armchair (Great Chair), Norwich or Lebanon, Connecticut, 1670-1710; ash and maple. *The Art Insti-* tute of Chicago, Wesley M. Dixon, Jr. Fund, Chicago, Illinois.

170. Highchair for child, Pennsylvania, 1740-1775; walnut. *The Art Institute of Chicago, gift of the Barker Welfare Foundation, Chicago, Illinois.*

171. Side chair, William Savery, Philadelphia, Pennsylvania, 1746-1760; maple. *The Art Institute of Chicago, gift of the Antiquarian Society, Chicago, Illinois.*

172. Side chair, Eliphalet or Aaron Chapin, East Windsor or Hartford, Connecticut, circa 1771-1790; mahogany with white pine and yellow pine. *The Art Institute of Chicago, gift of the Antiquarian Society, Chicago, Illinois.*

173

174

175

176

177

178

Vernacular Styles, 1791-1914

The great variety of the eighteenth century gradually decreases with developing mass production. By the 1870s, factories replace the efforts of most local craftsmen.

The early nineteenth century includes variations of many styles. Chests and tables still occur in the Medieval Style. Simple beds follow the seventeenth- and eighteenth-century form. Descendants of Spanish, Dutch, and German emigrants continue their distinctive styles. Adaptations of the Queen Anne, Chippendale, and Federal styles continue in isolated areas. Shakers produce simple designs into the early nineteenth century in their distinctive style.

Designs are carved with less frequency, as training and skills decline. Decoration increasingly is achieved by red, blue, yellow, or white paint, by simulating mahogany and maple grains, or by working simple designs into wet paint. By the 1830s, stencil decoration is common. Chairs by the Hitchcock factory and others gradually complement those in the Windsor Style, as furniture-production becomes an industry.

Rustic furniture of tree limbs with the bark intact evolves in the mid-nineteenth century as one of the styles for furniture in rural areas, mountain lodges, or informal rooms.

1. **Broken-arch pediment**
2. **Face (dial and spandrels)**
3. **Red and brown paint**
4. **Scalloped apron in Queen Anne Style**
5. **Yellow and brown paint**
6. **Writing surface**
7. **Drawers**
8. **Cabriole leg of Queen Anne Style**
9. **Low-post bedstead (wooden frame)**
10. **Headboard**
11. **Rope**
12. **Finial**
13. **Ovolo molding with egg-and-dart motif**
14. **Blind Chinese fret**
15. **Muntin**
16. **Inlaid festoon in Federal Style**
17. **Serpentine curve**
18. **Two-relief carved scallop shells of Queen Anne Style**
19. **Claw-and-ball foot of Chippendale Style**
20. **Hickory with bark intact**
21. **Shaped-oak back and seat**

173. Clock, Silas Hoadley, Plymouth, Connecticut, 1813-circa 1823; white pine painted red and brown. *The Art Institute of Chicago, gift of Marshall Field, Charles C. Haffner III, Mrs. Burton W. Hales, Mrs. C. Phillip Miller, Mrs. Clive Runnells, and Mrs. Frank L. Sulzberger, Chicago, Illinois.*

174. Writing stand, New England, 1815-1840; maple and white pine painted yellow and brown. *The Art Insti-tute of Chicago, Bessie Bennett Fund, Chicago, Illinois.*

175. Bedstead, Massachusetts, 1800-1850; ash. *The Henry Francis du Pont Winterthur Museum, gift of Joseph Downs, Winterthur, Delaware.*

176. Desk and bookcase, John Shearer, Martinsburg, West Virginia, 1801; cherry, walnut, oak, mulberry. *The Museum of Early Southern Decorative Arts, Winston-Salem, North Carolina.*

177. Armchair, northeastern United States, 1891-1910; various woods. *The Art Institute of Chicago, restricted gift of Jeffrey Shedd, Chicago, Illinois.*

178. Rocking chair, southern Ohio, 1890-1910; hickory frame, oak seat, back, and rockers. *The Art Institute of Chicago, gift of Mr. and Mrs. Robert A. Kubicek, Chicago, Illinois.*

179

180

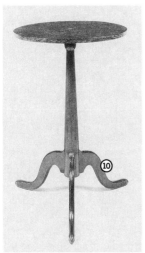

181

182

183

Shaker Style, 1800-1914

Efficient design and effective craftsmanship support principles of the United Society of Believers in Christ's Second Appearing. In 1774, nine members of the celibate sect that would become known as "Shakers," because of movements during ritual dances used in their worship, came to America from England. Conversions reached a peak in the 1840s, with about 6,000 members in communal centers from New England and the South to the Midwest.

Shaker furniture design generally follows early–nineteenth-century simple traditions familiar to the membership. Shakers made most of their furniture for dormitories and workshops, but in Mount Lebanon, New York, they made chairs and stools for public sale in the late nineteenth and early twentieth centuries. Later furniture also includes simplified motifs from sophisticated styles.

Shaker practicality encouraged such features as low-backed chairs that could be stored under dining tables, wheels on beds, and storage drawers built into walls. Early furniture is painted. By the mid-nineteenth century, stains, clear varnish, and shellac enchance grain and color of woods, which are functional as well as decorative. Easily shaped hickory or oak serves as chair slats, durable maple is used for drawer knobs, and dense cherry for table tops. Other woods include butternut, chestnut, pear, and walnut, as well as easily worked pine. Slight differences between various Shaker workshops are particularly evident in chairs through finial design, number and design of slats, and the varied use of straw, reed, or tape for seats.

1. Low-post bedstead (wooden frame)
2. Acorn-shaped finial
3. Headboard
4. Side rail
5. Footboard
6. Maple wheel
7. Drawer with knob handle
8. Slide for work surface
9. Bracket foot of Queen Anne Style
10. Cabriole leg of Queen Anne Style
11. Slat back
12. Splint seat
13. Rush seat

179. Bedstead, Mount (New) Lebanon, New York, Shaker Community, 1800-1830; chestnut posts, pine footboard, headboard, and rails, maple wheels. *The Henry Francis du Pont Winterthur Museum, gift of Miss Helen Brown, Miss Margaret Brown, and Miss Pauline Brown, Winterthur, Delaware.*

180. Desk, unidentified Shaker Community, United States, 1800-1850; ash, pine. *The Henry Francis du Pont Winterthur Museum, Winterthur, Delaware.*

181. Stand, attributed to Enfield, Connecticut, Shaker Community, 1790-1830; cherry. *The Henry Francis du Pont Winterthur Museum, Winterthur, Delaware.*

182. Rocking chair, attributed to Mount (New) Lebanon, New York, Shaker Community, 1800-1830; birch, maple. *The Henry Francis du Pont Winterthur Museum, Winterthur, Delaware; gift of the Halcyon Foundation, the American Museum in Britain, Claverton Manor, Bath, England.*

183. Dining chair, Mount (New) Lebanon, New York, Shaker Community (label), 1873-circa 1883; maple. *The Art Institute of Chicago, gift of the Antiquarian Society through the Mrs. Len H. Small Fund, Chicago, Illinois.*

184

185

186

187

188

189

Windsor Style furniture parts interlock for strength through tension. Side chairs complement armchairs by the 1770s, and settees are popular by the 1790s, with occasional stools and tables.

Woods selected for function include hard oak for arms or crests, dense maple for legs, supple hickory and birch for spindles or crests, and soft ash, tulip, or pine for shaped seats. By the mid-nineteenth century, color and grain are decorative features, instead of red, yellow, blue-green or white paint. Rare eighteenth-century Windsors with cabriole legs and pad feet are made of walnut, a wood recurring in the mid-twentieth century.

Craftsmen specialize in Windsors until the early nineteenth century, by making or buying interchangeable parts. After nineteenth-century factory production, independent craftsmen return in the mid-twentieth century.

Windsor furniture evolved in or near London between 1710 and 1720. It is identified from this period to the early nineteenth century with garden furniture at Windsor castle. Rural English craftsmen were developing the style by the second quarter of the eighteenth century, and it reached Philadelphia at mid-century. By the Revolution, variations occur in New York City and Newport. After the Revolution, craftsmen made Windsors throughout the new nation, and the furniture is common for elegant, as well as plain, houses and for gardens. Decorative turnings are baluster shapes in the eighteenth century, bamboo shapes after the Revolution, concentric rings in the mid-nineteenth century, and disappear in the twentieth.

1. **Crest rail with volutes**
2. **Doric column**
3. **Baluster turning**
4. **Brace**
5. **Blue-green paint over surface**
6. **Medial and side stretchers**
7. **Cabriole leg and pad foot of Queen Anne Style**
8. **Bamboo-shaped turnings**
9. **Brown and red paint**
10. **Gilt stencil decoration**
11. **Varnish finish**
12. **Trestle base**

184. Windsor armchair, Philadelphia, Pennsylvania, 1761-1770; tulip seat, maple legs, hickory spindles, oak arms, painted blue-green. *The Art Institute of Chicago, gift of Elizabeth R. Vaughan, Chicago, Illinois.*

185. Windsor armchair, Philadelphia, Pennsylvania, 1760-1775; walnut. *The Art Institute of Chicago, gift of Joyce Martin Brown, Marshall Field, Mrs. Harold T. Martin, Melinda Martin Vance, and Mary Waller Langhorne Fund, Chicago, Illinois.*

186. Windsor settee, probably Pennsylvania, 1785-1800; oak spindles, crest rail, arms, tulip seat, maple legs, stretchers, and rear stiles; painted brown over red and blue-green. *The Yale University Art Gallery, Mabel Brady Garvan Collection, New Haven, Connecticut.*

187. Windsor rocking chair, New England, 1830-1850; hickory or oak spindles, pine seat, maple legs and arms, painted brown and red with gilt stencil decoration. *Greenfield Village and Henry Ford Museum, Dearborn, Michigan. (Accession No. 24. 111. 120.)*

188. Windsor side chair for child, probably New England, 1880-1890; oak rail, ash seat, birch spindles. *Mark Twain Memorial, Hartford, Connecticut.*

189. Windsor side chair, George Nakashima, New Hope, Pennsylvania, 1988 (design introduced circa 1962); walnut with hickory spindles. *The Art Institute of Chicago, Raymond W. Garbe fund in honor of Carl A. Erikson, Sr., Chicago, Illinois.*

190

191

192

193

194

195

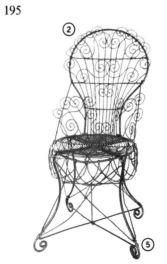

196

Windsors graced gardens and houses until the early nineteenth century. Chairs made in factories replaced Windsors indoors by mid-century as a new and substantial furniture became available for outdoors.

Iron production had greatly advanced from the late eighteenth to the mid-nineteenth centuries in England. Costs were reduced and casting improved for delicacy in details and greater size in parts. Legs, backs, and seats could be made as standard parts, shipped, and assembled with screws. Occasional furniture in the Gothic Style led to widespread production of tables, chairs, and settees in the Rococo Revival Style. General popularity with this style led to designs in all of the later styles. They were disseminated from England and within America, as the product of one manufacturer easily served as the pattern for another's mold.

Wire production encouraged a new kind of furniture by the 1870s. Interlaced designs provided both strength and decoration in chairs, stands, and settees.

Native willow and imported rattan offered materials for a wide range of simple and elaborate forms after the War Between the States. The furniture also served informally in houses by the late nineteenth and early twentieth centuries.

Rustic furniture of gnarled tree limbs with the bark intact gained popularity at mid-century with the Naturalistic Style. Most of the survivals are from the late nineteenth century, when the approach became common, not only in gardens, but also in mountain lodges and in vernacular furniture throughout the United States.

1. **Gothic Revival Style**
2. **Rococo Revival Style**
3. **Cabriole leg**
4. **Renaissance Revival Style**
5. **Scroll foot**
6. **Classical influence**
7. **Lancet arch of Gothic Revival Style**
8. **Saltire stretcher**
9. **Japanese design influence**

190. Settee, probably New York, circa 1836; cast-iron. *Historic Hudson Valley, Tarrytown, New York.*

191. Side chair, Robert Wood and Company, Philadelphia, Pennsylvania, 1850-1860; cast-iron. *Greenfield Village and Henry Ford Museum, Dearborn, Michigan. (Accession No. 65. 118. 3.)*

192. Table, United States, 1850-1870; cast-iron. *The Metropolitan Museum of Art, Anonymous Gift Fund, 1968, New York, New York.*

193. Urn, Van Dorn Iron Works, Cleveland, Ohio, 1850-1885; cast-iron. *The Metropolitan Museum of Art, Edgar J. Kaufmann, Jr. Charitable Foundation Fund, 1969, New York, New York.*

194. Settee, Colt Willow Ware Works, Hartford, Connecticut, circa 1855-1873; willow. *The Wadsworth Atheneum, Colt Collection, Hartford Connecticut.*

195. Side chair, United States, 1875-1880; wire. *Greenfield Village and Henry Ford Museum, Dearborn Michigan. (Accession No. 58. 57. 1.)*

196. Settee, the Kramer Brothers, Dayton Ohio, 1905-1925; cast-iron. *The Art Institute of Chicago, gift of the Antiquarian Society through Mrs. Burton W. Hales, Chicago, Illinois.*

Publications in the following list are selective but include the major references available for style, technology, and terminology. They are arranged in two general categories: Periodicals and Books, Articles, and Manuscripts. In the latter category, articles may be from journals or magazines cited among the Periodicals, but they are listed separately for their significance to the theme of this book. Annotations occur either to clarify the scope of a publication or to alert the reader to unusual circumstances.

The category of Books, Articles, and Manuscripts is divided into several groups. One is Background Sources: Architecture and Design. Another is General Sources: American Furniture. It includes publications covering more than one region and is followed by alphabetized sources for the regions of the Hawaiian Islands, the Mid-Atlantic, the Midwest, New England, the South, the Southwest, and the West. Colonies or states are grouped in the traditional way. References to Maryland and upstate New York remain, for example, under the Mid-Atlantic region, even though Maryland drew closer to the South in the nineteenth century and upstate New York often differs from the interests of New York City.

Periodicals

The American Art Journal, 1969—
Antiques (The Magazine Antiques), 1922—
Antiques World, 1978-1982
Arts and Antiques, 1978—
Furniture History, 1965—
The Journal of Early Southern Decorative Arts, 1975—
The Journal of Decorative and Propaganda Arts, 1875-1945, 1986—
Nineteenth Century, 1975-1984
The V & A Album, I (1982)—
Victoria and Albert Museum Yearbook, One (1969)-Four (1973)
Winterthur Portfolio, I (1964)—

Books, Articles, and Manuscripts

Background Sources: Architecture and Design

Agius, Pauline. *British Furniture: 1880-1915.* Woodbridge, Suffolk, England: Baron Publishing for the Antique Collectors' Club, 1978. Illustrated survey of mass-produced and custom-designed furniture.

Antique Collectors' Club. *Pictorial Dictionary of British 19th Century Furniture Design.* Introduction by Edward Joy. Woodbridge, Suffolk, England: Baron Publishing for the Antique Collectors' Club, 1977. Illustrations from nineteenth-century-design books, price guides, and catalogues grouped by form and the identified source discussed in the excellent introduction; the publication is an essential reference for the English background of American nineteenth-century furniture.

Aslin, Elizabeth. *The Aesthetic Movement, Prelude to Art Nouveau.* New York: Frederick A. Praeger, 1969. Essential reference for the English background of American Art Furniture in the 1870s and 1880s.

————. *E. W. Godwin: Furniture and Interior Decoration.* London: John Murray, 1986. Authoritative study of a major force in the English Aesthetic Movement which influenced American furniture of the 1870s and 1880s.

————. *Nineteenth Century English Furniture.* London: Faber, 1962. Excellent concise review of styles.

Beyer, Victor; Hiesinger, Kathryn B.; Moulin, Jean-Marie; and Rishel, Joseph; exhibition organizers for the Philadelphia Museum of Art, The Detroit Institute of Arts, and the Musée du Louvre. *The Second Empire, 1852-1870: Art in France under Napoleon III.* Philadelphia: The Philadelphia Museum of Art, 1978. See especially entries by various authors for "Interior Views," pages 77-82, and "Furniture," pages 94-114. Detailed and accurate information unavailable elsewhere that is significant for the analysis of contemporary American styles.

Blumenson, John J.-G. *Identifying American Architecture: A Pictorial Guide to Styles and Terms, 1600-1945.* Nashville: American Association for State and Local History, 1977. Introduction to architectural styles, that is comparable to this guide for furniture, with pictorial glossary of classical and other architectural motifs often adapted to furniture.

Brandt, Frederick R. *Late 19th and Early 20th Century Decorative Arts: The Sydney and Frances Lewis Collection in the Virginia Museum of Fine Arts.* Richmond: The Virginia Museum of Fine Arts, 1985. Nationally pre-eminent collection stressing European furniture but including a few American examples; the collection is especially informative for the background of American furniture of the 1920s and the 1930s; excellent commentaries and color illustrations.

Brunhammer, Yvonne. *The Art Deco Style.* London: Academy Editions, 1983. Well-illustrated survey of European movement only.

Bunston, J., compiler. *English Furniture Designs, 1800-1914: A Bibliography of 120 Pattern Books and Trade Catalogues in the Library of the Victoria and Albert Museum.* London: The Museum and National Art Library, no date.

Chinnery, Victor. *Oak Furniture: The British Tradition: A History of Early Furniture in the British Isles and New England.* Woodbridge, Suffolk, England: Baron Publishing for the Antique Collectors' Club, 1979. Reprinted 1984; reprinted 1986 with additional pictorial index. New England furniture briefly discussed and date or origin should be verified, but the context with British sixteenth- and seventeenth-century furniture is informative.

Comino, Mary. *Gimson and the Barnsleys: "Wonderful furniture of a commonplace kind."* New York: Van Nostrand Reinhold Co., Inc., 1982. United Kingdom edition published 1980 by Evans Brothers Ltd. Through the lives and furniture of Ernest Gimson and the brothers Ernest and Sidney Barnsley, the author offers a unique insight into the English Arts and Crafts Movement.

Eames, Penelope. *Furniture in England, France, and the Netherlands from the Twelfth to the Fifteenth Century.* Leeds: The Furniture History Society, 1977. Published as volume XIII of *Furniture History,* the journal of the Furniture History Society. Authoritative and documented study of the use and appearance of furniture by type; illustrated by line drawings and photographic illustrations; excellent bibliography.

Ellsworth, Robert Hatfield. *Chinese Furniture: Hardwood Examples of the Ming and Early Ch'ing Dynasties.* New York: Random House, 1971. Authoritative presentation of stylistic and technical information; excellent illustrations.

Evans, Nancy Goyne. "A History and Background of English Windsor Furniture." *Furniture History* XV (1979): pages 24-53, plates 68A-95B. Credible speculation that the Windsor form emerged during the early eighteenth century in turners' shops in London and nearby; evolution of Windsors documented to the early nineteenth century; essential reference for background of American Windsors.

Garner, Philippe. *Twentieth-Century Furniture.* New York: Van Nostrand Reinhold Co., 1980. Innovative themes and designers among Europeans and Americans analyzed by decades in a well-illustrated survey.

Gilbert, Christopher. *The Life and Works of Thomas Chippendale,* 2 volumes. London: Studio Vista, in association with Christie, Manson & Woods Ltd., 1978. Documented and illustrated study with a chapter about *The Gentleman and Cabinet-Maker's Director* (volume I, chapter 4, pages 65-107) and useful discussions of topics pertinent to the operation of the shop; letters, bills, and other documentation for furniture offer further insights into the styles of the period.

Gillow Archives, 1731-1932 [101 microfilm reels], 1971. These unique records of a major English furniture firm minutely document styles there over two centuries. The Art Institute of Chicago and the Winterthur Museum are two libraries in the United States with a microfilm of the original records in London at the City of Westminster Libraries, Archives Section.

Hardy, John. "Rococo Furniture and Carving." In *Rococo Art and Design in Hogarth's England,* pages 153-188. London: The Victoria and Albert Museum, 1984. The publication generally and Hardy's contribution specifically are essential background for American furniture from the 1740s to the 1780s.

Hayward, Helena, editor. *World Furniture.* New York and Toronto: McGraw-Hill Book Co., 1965. Reprinted 1973. Written by specialists, the book is the most authoritative survey published.

Heskett, John. *German Design, 1870-1918.* New York: Taplinger Publishing

Co., 1986. Furniture included in survey of concepts, designers, and objects; background for development of Bauhaus and American furniture 1930s to present.

Horn, Richard. *Memphis: Objects, Furniture, and Patterns.* Second revised edition. Philadelphia: Running Press, 1986.

McFadden, David Revere. Exhibition administrator for the Cooper-Hewitt Museum, The Smithsonian Institution's National Museum of Design, New York City, and The Carnegie Museum of Art, Pittsburgh. *Courts and Colonies: The William and Mary Style in Holland, England, and America.* Seattle and London: University of Washington Press, 1988. Exhibition organization and catalogue essays by Reinier Baarsen, "The Court Style in Holland;" Elaine Evans Dee, "Printed Sources for the William and Mary Style;" Gervase Jackson-Stops, "The Court Style in Britain;" and Phillip M. Johnston, "The William and Mary Style in America." Catalogue entries by Dee, Johnston, Deborah Sampson Shinn, and Linda Rosenfeld Shulsky. Essential reference for the European background and American evolution of the style.

Macquoid, Percy, and Edwards, Ralph. *The Dictionary of English Furniture from the Middle Ages to the Late Georgian Period.* 3 volumes. Second revised edition by Ralph Edwards. London: Country Life, 1954. Illustrated survey of sophisticated and vernacular furniture with reliable definitions of terms.

Mang, Karl. *History of Modern Furniture.* Translated by John William Gabriel. New York: Harry N. Abrams, Inc., 1979. European and American innovative concepts in design and fabrication traced from the 1840s to the 1970s.

Richter, Gisela Marie Augusta. *The Furniture of the Greeks, Etruscans, and Romans.* London: Phaidon, 1966. The most authoritative survey published.

Shixiang, Wang. *Classic Chinese Furniture: Ming and Early Qing Dynasties.* Translated by Sarah Handler and the author. London: Han-Shan Tang Ltd., 1986. A catalogue of 175 objects in China includes color photographs (usually with details) and a commentary introduced by essays about woods, construction, etc.

Thornton, Peter. *Authentic Decor: The Domestic Interior, 1620-1920.* London: Weidenfeld and Nicolson, 1984. Seven periods documented by 532 carefully selected contemporary paintings, water colors, prints, and drawings with an informative explanatory caption for each; includes northern Europe, Great Britain, Scandinavia, and the United States; informative for documenting and dating sophisticated and vernacular furniture styles.

_____. *Seventeenth-Century Interior Decoration in England, France and Holland.* New Haven and London: Yale University Press, for the Paul Mellon Centre for Studies in British Art, 1978. Authoritative and well illustrated; chapters on beds (VII), upholstered seat-furniture (VIII), tables and cupboards (IX), and such miscellaneous forms as screens, looking glasses, and ornamental cabinets (X).

Toher, Jennifer. "Furniture and Interior Decoration." In *Encyclopedia of Art Deco,* Alistair Duncan, editor. New York: E. P. Dutton, 1988. Excellent analytical and illustrative survey of the varied movements, including the United States.

Varnedoe, Kirk. *Vienna 1900: Art, Architecture & Design.* New York: The Museum of Modern Art, 1986. Chapter entitled "Design" includes furniture with other decorative arts; offers insights into innovative American designs of the early twentieth century.

Victoria and Albert Museum. Introduction by Roy Strong. *British Art and Design 1900-1960.* Second edition. London: The Museum, 1984. Furniture included with a survey of museum collections.

Ward-Jackson, Peter. *English Furniture Designs of the Eighteenth Century.* London: Her Majesty's Stationery Office, 1958. Essential for study of styles in the British Isles and North America.

Weisberg, Gabriel P. *Art Nouveau Bing: Paris Style 1900.* New York: Harry N. Abrams, Inc., in association with the Smithsonian Institution Traveling Exhibition Service (SITES), 1986. Background of the retail shop, the designers, the workshops producing objects, and the furniture sold (among other objects); authoritative and profusely illustrated study; excellent bibliography; essential background for American furniture 1896-1914.

General Sources: American Furniture

Ames, Kenneth L. "What is neo-grec?" and "Sitting in (Neo-Grec) Style." *Nineteenth Century* 2, nos. 2, 3-4 (Summer, Autumn 1976): pages 13-21, 51-58.

Bates, Elizabeth Bidwell, and Fairbanks, Jonathan L. *American Furniture, 1620 to the Present.* New York: R. Marek, 1981.

Bishop, Robert. *Centuries and Styles of the American Chair, 1640-1970.* New York: E. P. Dutton & Co., 1972.

Blaser, Werner. *Mies van der Rohe: Furniture and Interiors.* Woodbury, New York: Barron's Education Series, 1982.

Cathers, David M. *Furniture of the American Arts and Crafts Movement.* New York: New Amsterdam Library, 1981. Emphasis on Gustav Stickley's furniture with comment on Leopold Stickley and Elbert Hubbard; discussion of furniture by form.

Clark, Robert Judson, et al. *The Arts and Crafts Movement in America,* Princeton: Princeton University Press, 1972.

Cooke, Edward S. *New American Furniture.* Boston: The Museum of Fine Arts, 1989. Discussion of twenty-five artisans the author considers in the second generation of "studio makers."

_____, editor. *Upholstery in America and Europe from the Seventeenth Century to World War I.* New York and London: W. W. Norton and Co., for the Barra Foundation, 1987. Twenty illustrated and documented articles by Cooke and others.

Cooper, Wendy A. *In Praise of America: American Decorative Arts, 1650-1830: Fifty Years of Discovery Since the 1929 Girl Scouts Loan Exhibition.* New York: Alfred A. Knopf, 1980.

Davies, Karen. *At Home in Manhattan: Modern Decorative Arts, 1925 to the Depression.* New Haven: Yale University Art Gallery, 1983. Furniture included in a documented and illustrated survey.

Dietz, Ulysses G. *Century of Revivals: Nineteenth-Century American Furniture from the Collection of the Newark Museum.* Newark, New Jersey: The Museum, 1982.

Domergue, Denise. *Artists Design Furniture.* New York: Harry N. Abrams, Inc., 1984. Furniture designed by sixty-seven artists since World War II with their comments on their approaches.

Downs, Joseph. *American Furniture: Queen Anne and Chippendale Periods in the Henry Francis du Pont Winterthur Museum.* New York: The Macmillan Co., 1952.

Drexler, Arthur. *Charles Eames Furniture from the Design Collection.* New York: The Museum of Modern Art, 1973.

Dubrow, Eileen and Richard. *American Furniture of the 19th Century, 1840-1880.* Exton, Pennsylvania: Schiffer Publications, 1983.

Duncan, Alastair. *American Art Deco.* New York: Harry N. Abrams, Inc., 1986. The chapter on furniture, pages 31-65, includes commissioned and mass-produced objects.

Evans, Nancy Goyne. "Design Sources for Windsor Furniture, Part I: The Eighteenth Century," *Antiques* CXXXIII (1988), pages 282-297.

_____. "Design Sources for Windsor Furniture, Part II: The Early Nineteenth Century," *Antiques* CXXXIII (1988), pages 1128-1143.

_____. "Striking Accents: Ornamental Hardwoods in the American Windsor," *Maine Antique Digest,* December, 1988, pages 8c-11c.

Fales, Dean A. *American Painted Furniture.* New York: Dutton, 1972. Includes bibliography.

Flanigan, J. Michael, with introductory essays by Wendy A. Cooper, Morrison H. Heckscher, and Gregory R. Weidman. *American Furniture from the Kauffman Collection.* Washington: The National Gallery of Art, 1986. Color illustrations, technical notes, and commentaries for 101 quality objects collected by Mr. and Mrs. George Kauffman; emphasis on the late eighteenth and early nineteenth centuries; includes earlier furniture.

Forman, Benno M. *American Seating Furniture, 1630-1730: An Interpretive Catalogue.* Winterthur, Delaware: W. W. Norton & Co., for the Winterthur Museum, 1987.

Hanks, David A. *The Decorative Designs of Frank Lloyd Wright.* New York: E. P. Dutton, 1979. Includes furniture.

_____, with essays by Rodris Roth and Page Talbot. *Innovative Furniture in America: From 1880 to the Present.* New York: Horizon Press, 1981. Includes bibliography.

————— , with Jennifer Toher and an essay by Jeffrey L. Meikle. *Donald Deskey: Decorative Designs and Interiors.* New York: E. P. Dutton, 1987. Life and work of a major designer from the 1920s to the 1950s.

————— , and Peirce, Donald C. *The Virginia Carroll Crawford Collection: American Decorative Arts, 1825-1917.* Atlanta: The High Museum of Art, 1983. Includes furniture with brief commentaries for objects.

Heckscher, Morrison H. *American Furniture in the Metropolitan Museum of Art: Late Colonial Period, The Queen Anne and Chippendale Periods.* New York: The Museum and Random House, 1985. Concise technical notes and excellent illustrations for 213 objects.

————— . "Philadelphia Chippendale: The Influence of the *Director* in America," *Furniture History* XXI (1985), pages 283-288, figures 1-23.

Herman, Lloyd E., with research by Dezso Sekely. *A Modern Consciousness: D. J. De Pree, Florence Knoll.* Washington, D. C.: Smithsonian Institution Press, for the National Collection of Fine Arts, 1975. Careers of two people significant in two major firms in post World War II furniture, Herman Miller, Inc., and Knoll International.

Hewitt, Benjamin A.; Kane, Patricia E.; and Ward, Gerald W. R. *The Work of Many Hands: Card Tables in Federal America, 1790-1820.* New Haven: The Yale University Art Gallery, 1982. Analysis of card tables for local and regional features.

Hiesinger, Kathryn B., and Marcus, George H., editors. *Design Since 1945.* Philadelphia: The Philadelphia Museum of Art, 1983. Furniture by Americans included in an illustrated international survey with essays by designers and biographies of them; bibliographies included for the designers and concepts.

Hillier, Bevis. "Furniture." In *Art Deco,* pages 52-63. Minneapolis: The Minneapolis Institute of Arts, 1971.

Howe, Katherine S., and Warren, David B., with introduction by Jane B. Davies. *The Gothic-Revival Style in America, 1830-1870.* Houston: The Museum of Fine Arts, Houston, 1976. Unique and authoritative study.

Hummel, Charles F. *A Winterthur Guide to American Chippendale Furniture: Middle Atlantic and Southern Colonies.* New York: Crown Publishers, Inc., for Rutledge Books, 1976.

Israel Sack, Inc. *Opportunities in American Antiques.* New York: Israel Sack, Inc., 1957— . Occasional brochures with illustrations and comments about furniture for sale; objects date from the seventeenth, eighteenth, and early nineteenth centuries. Brochures collected and republished in book form as *American Antiques from Israel Sack Collection.* Washington, D. C.: Highland House Publishers, Inc., vol. I (1969)— .

Johnson, Marilynn; Schwartz, Marvin D.; Boorsch, Suzanne; and Tracy, Berry B. *19th-Century America: Furniture and Other Decorative Arts: An Exhibition in Celebration of the Hundredth Anniversary of the Metropolitan Museum of Art,* April 6-September 7, 1970. Furniture texts by Johnson; other decorative arts by Schwartz and Boorsch; introduction by Berry B. Tracy.

————— . "The Artful Interior" and "Art Furniture: Wedding the Beautiful to the Useful." In *In Pursuit of Beauty: Americans and the Aesthetic Movement,* New York: The Metropolitan Museum of Art and Rizzoli International Publications, 1986.

Johnston, Phillip M. "The William and Mary Style in America." In *Courts and Colonies: The William and Mary Style in Holland, England, and America,* pages 62-79, and pertinent catalogue entries. Seattle and London: University of Washington Press, 1988. Essential reference for evolution of the style in America.

Kane, Patricia E. *300 Years of Seating Furniture: Chairs and Beds from the Mabel Brady Garvan and Other Collections at Yale University.* Boston: The New York Graphic Society, 1976.

Kaplan, Wendy, editor. *"The Art that is Life": The Arts & Crafts Movement in America, 1875-1920.* Boston: The Museum of Fine Arts, 1987. Furniture included in several essays as a facet of the movement.

Kassay, John. *The Book of Shaker Furniture.* Amherst: University of Massachusetts Press, 1980.

Kirk, John T. *American Furniture & the British Tradition to 1830.* New York: Knopf, with distribution by Random House, 1982.

Levy, Bernard and S. Dean. *An American Tea Party: An Exhibition of Colonial Tea and Breakfast Tables, 1715-1783.* New York: Bernard & S. Dean Levy, Inc., 1988. Thirty-eight examples from public and private collections; Exhibition Catalog (October 19-November 5, 1988).

Madigan, Mary Jean Smith. *Eastlake-Influenced American Furniture, 1870-1890.* Yonkers: The Hudson-River Museum, 1973.

Meader, Robert F. *Illustrated Guide to Shaker Furniture.* New York: Dover Publications, Inc., 1972.

Monkhouse, Christopher P., and Michie, Thomas S., with the assistance of John M. Carpenter. *American Furniture in Pendleton House.* Providence, Rhode Island: Rhode Island School of Design, 1986. Illustrations, technical notes, and essays for 164 objects dating from the seventeenth century to the present in a house built as a setting for the collection; excellent bibliography.

Montgomery, Charles F. *American Furniture: The Federal Period in the Henry Francis du Pont Winterthur Museum.* New York: Viking Press, 1966.

Morse, John D., editor. *Country Cabinetwork and Simple City Furniture.* Charlottesville: University Press of Virginia, for the Henry Francis du Pont Winterthur Museum, 1970. Articles by seven specialists about vernacular furniture.

Naeve, Milo M. *The Classical Presence in American Art.* Chicago: The Art Institute of Chicago, 1978. Illustrated essay about Greek and Roman influences on American art, including furniture, from the seventeenth to the twentieth centuries.

_____ . "American Arts: Furniture." In *A Decade of Decorative Arts: The Antiquarian Society of the Art Institute of Chicago.* Chicago: The Art Institute of Chicago, 1986. Essays on twelve eighteenth- and nineteenth-century objects exceptional in quality and frequently unique that are gifts from the Society to the Art Institute. In this study, the objects include nos. 18, 21, 28, 38, 107, 109.

Nordness, Lee. *Objects: USA.* New York: A Studio Book, Viking Press, 1970. Survey of crafts at the time of publication through innovative objects; biographies of craftsmen.

Ostergard, Derek E., editor, with essays by Ostergard and others. *Bent Wood and Metal Furniture: 1850-1946.* New York: The American Federation of Arts, 1987. Illustrations, technical notes, and commentaries on European

and American examples; appendix of manufacturers (1849-1914), glossary, and bibliography.

Phillips, Lisa. *Shape and Environment: Furniture by American Architects.* New York: The Whitney Museum of American Art, Fairfield County, 1982. General bibliography and bibliographies for each architect included.

_____ . *High Styles: Twentieth-Century Design.* New York: The Whitney Museum of American Art, in association with Summit Books, 1985. Essays by Phillips and five others illustrating and analyzing eclectic as well as innovative styles.

Pilgrim, Dianne H. "The Decorative Art: The Domestic Environment." In *The American Renaissance: 1876-1917*, pages 110-151. Brooklyn: The Brooklyn Museum, 1979. Furniture surveyed with other subjects.

_____ . "Design for the Machine." In *The Machine Age in America. 1918-1941*, pages 271-337. New York: The Brooklyn Museum, in association with Harry N. Abrams, Inc., 1986. Emphasis on mass-production with comment on furniture.

Quimby, Ian M. G., editor. *Arts of the Anglo-American Community in the Seventeenth Century.* Charlottesville: University Press of Virginia, for the Henry Francis du Pont Winterthur Museum, 1975. See especially Patricia E. Kane, "The Seventeenth-Century Furniture of the Connecticut Valley: The Hadley Chest Reappraised," pages 79-122; Robert F. Trent, "The Joiners and Joinery of Middlesex County, Massachusetts, 1630-1730," pages 123-148; and other articles presenting the background of American furniture in English and Dutch furniture.

Randall, Richard H. *American Furniture in the Museum of Fine Arts, Boston.* Boston: The Museum, 1965.

Renwick Gallery of the National Collection of Fine Arts, Smithsonian Institution, Washington, D. C., and the Minnesota Museum of Art. *Woodenworks: George Nakashima, Sam Maloof, Wharton Esherick, Arthur Espenet Carpenter, and Wendell Castle.* St. Paul: The Minnesota Museum of Art, 1972.

Rodriguez Roque, Oswaldo. *American Furniture at Chipstone.* Introduction by Stanley Stone. Madison: University of Wisconsin Press, 1984. An illustrated catalogue of the collection of Mr. and Mrs. Stanley Stone at Chipstone, their residence in Milwaukee; the collection includes American furniture before 1815 and emphasizes the Queen Anne and Chippendale periods, especially in Rhode Island.

Sack, Albert. *Fine Points of Furniture: Early American.* New York: Crown Publishers, Inc., 1950. Unique guide to quality in furniture through the early nineteenth century.

Santore, Charles. *The Windsor Style in America: A Pictorial Study of the History and Regional Characteristics of the Most Popular Furniture Form of 18th Century America, 1730-1830.* Philadelphia: Running Press, 1981. Includes checklist of craftsmen.

————. *The Windsor Style in America: Volume II.* Philadelphia: Running Press, 1987. Remarks on regional variations with checklist of makers and illustrations of labels or brands.

Saunders, Richard. *Collector's Guide to American Wicker Furniture.* New York: Hearst Books, 1983.

Schwartz, Marvin D. *Chairs, Tables, Sofas & Beds.* New York: Alfred A. Knopf, 1982. Volume I of the Knopf Collectors' Guide to American Antiques includes 347 illustrations organized chronologically by type.

Semowich, Charles J. *American Furniture Craftsmen Working Prior to 1920: An Annotated Bibliography.* Westport, Connecticut, and London, England: Greenwood Press, 1984. Includes lists of pertinent trade catalogues, furniture periodicals, and manuscript collections.

Smith, Paul J. *New Handmade Furniture: American Furniture Makers Working in Hardwood.* New York: The American Craft Museum, 1979. Includes Stewart Paul, Lee M. Rohde, Lee A. Schuette, Alan Siegel, John Snedicor, Michael Speaker, and Daniel Loomis Valenza.

————, with introductory essay about American crafts since the 1890s by Edward Lucie-Smith. *Craft Today: Poetry of the Physical.* New York: The American Craft Museum, 1986. Includes furniture with other objects, excellent chronology of events and major exhibitions in American crafts from 1851-1986, detailed biographies of craftsmen, a general bibliography, and a limited bibliography for furniture under the category "Wood."

Sprigg, June. *Shaker Design.* New York and London: The Whitney Museum of American Art, in association with W. W. Norton & Co., 1986. Concise discussion of furniture with selective bibliography.

Stephenson, Sue H. *Rustic Furniture.* New York: Van Nostrand Reinhold Company, 1979. Emphasis on nineteenth-century American versions with survey of European and Oriental background; includes techniques for making furniture.

Stone, Michael A. *Contemporary American Woodworkers.* Salt Lake City: Gibbs M. Smith, Inc., 1986. Illustrated commentary about Wharton Esherick, George Nakashima, Bob Stocksdale, Tage Frid, Sam Maloof, Arthur Espenet Carpenter, James Krenov, Wendell Castle, Garry Knox Bennett, and Jere Osgood.

Teller, Betty. "American Furniture in the Art Nouveau Style." In *Art & Antiques* 3, no. 3 (May-June 1980): pages 96-101. Foremost publication on the subject.

Venable, Charles L. *The Faith P. and Charles L. Bybee Collection of American Furniture.* Dallas, Texas: The Dallas Museum of Art, 1986. Collection includes eighteenth and early nineteenth centuries.

Voorsanger, Catherine Hoover. "Dictionary of Architects, Artisans, Artists, and Manufacturers." In *In Pursuit of Beauty: Americans and the Aesthetic Movement.* New York: The Metropolitan Museum of Art and Rizzoli International Publications, 1986. Includes significant innovators in furniture design and fabrication with an excellent bibliography for each entry.

Ward, Barbara, et al. *A Place for Everything: Chests and Boxes in Early Colonial America.* Winterthur: The Henry Francis du Pont Winterthur Museum, 1986. Ten seventeenth- and early eighteenth-century New England objects at Winterthur analyzed for origin, style, fabrication, and function by the class of 1987 Lois F. McNeil Fellows in the Winterthur Program in Early American Culture.

Ward, Gerald W. R. *American Case Furniture in the Mabel Brady Garvan and Other Collections at Yale University.* New Haven: The Yale University Art Gallery, 1988. Thorough comments with excellent illustrations.

Warren, David B. *Bayou Bend: American Furniture, Paintings, and Silver from the Bayou Bend Collection.* Houston: The Museum of Fine Artists, 1975.

Wilk, Christopher. *Marcel Breuer: Furniture and Interiors.* Introduction by J. Stewart Johnson. New York: The Museum of Modern Art, 1981. European and American careers treated separately with excellent illustrations and thorough documentation.

Regional Sources: Hawaiian Islands

Hackler, Rhoda E. A. *Koa Furniture of Hawaii.* Honolulu: University of Hawaii Department of Art, Partners, and the Daughters of Hawaii, 1981. Includes bibliography.

Jenkins, Irving. *Hawaiian Furniture and Hawaii's Cabinetmakers, 1820-1940.* Honolulu: Editions Ltd., for the Daughters of Hawaii, 1983. Includes bibliography.

Regional Sources: Mid-Atlantic

Blades, Margaret Bleeker. *Two Hundred Years of Chairs and Chairmaking: An Exhibition of Chairs from the Chester County Historical Society.* Edited by Ann Barton Brown. West Chester, Pennsylvania: The Chester County Historical Society, 1987.

Butler, Joseph T. *Sleepy Hollow Restorations: A Cross-Section of the Collection.* Tarrytown, New York: Sleepy Hollow Restorations, 1983. Includes furniture; illustrations with excellent technical notes.

Castle, Wendell, and Edman, David. *The Wendell Castle Book of Wood Lamination.* New York: Van Nostrand Reinhold, 1980.

de Julio, Mary Antoine. *German Folk Arts of New York State.* Albany, New York: The Albany Institute of History and Art, 1985. Furniture included with other arts; authoritative illustrated commentary.

Fabian, Monroe H. *The Pennsylvania-German Decorated Chest.* New York: Universe Books, 1978.

Failey, Dean F. *Long Island Is My Nation: The Decorative Arts and Craftsmen, 1640-1830.* Setauket, New York: The Society for the Preservation of Long Island Antiquities, 1977.

Forman, Benno M. "German Influences in Pennsylvania Furniture." In *Arts of the Pennsylvania Germans,* pages 102-170. Winterthur: W. W. Norton & Co., for the Henry Francis du Pont Winterthur Museum, 1983.

Garvan, Beatrice B. *Federal Philadelphia, 1785-1825: The Athens of the Western World.* Philadelphia: The Philadelphia Museum of Art, 1987. Furniture included with other arts and crafts.

_____ . *The Pennsylvania German Collection.* Philadelphia: The Philadelphia Museum of Art, 1982. Descriptive and technical Notes for furniture in the illustrated section devoted to the medium of wood; the collection is the most comprehensive.

_____ , and Hummel, Charles F., eds. *The Pennsylvania Germans: A Celebration of Their Arts, 1683-1850.* The Philadelphia Museum of Art and the Henry Francis du Pont Winterthur Museum, 1982. Contributions by Garvan and Hummel with seven other specialists; furniture included in topical essays.

Gilborn, Craig. *Adirondack Furniture and the Rustic Tradition.* New York: Abrams, 1987. Furniture made in the Adirondack Park and imported from Indiana, Ohio, Pennsylvania, and Ontario from the 1880s to the 1920s.

Griffith, Lee Ellen. *The Pennsylvania Spice Box: Paneled Doors and Secret Drawers.* West Chester, Pennsylvania: The Chester County Historical Society, 1986.

Hammel, Lisa. *Time and Defiance of Gravity: Recent Works by Wendell Castle.* Rochester, New York: The Memorial Art Gallery of the University of Rochester, 1986. Complete record through illustrations and accompanying notes of the thirteen clocks made by Castle in 1984 and 1985.

Hemphill, Christopher. "Against the Grain: The Art of Wendell Castle." *Town and Country,* 138 (May 1984): page 243 and subsequent pages. Excellent survey of Castle's career; includes eight color illustrations.

Hornor, William Macpherson, Jr. *Blue Book, Philadelphia Furniture: William Penn to George Washington with Special Reference to the Philadelphia Chippendale School.* Philadelphia: Privately printed, 1935. Second printing with index and revised captions, Washington, D.C.: Highland House Publishers, Inc., 1977.

Hummel, Charles F. *With Hammer in Hand: The Dominy Craftsmen of East*

Hampton, New York. Charlottesville: University Press of Virginia, for the Winterthur Museum, 1968. Furniture, tools, materials, and craft procedures of the Dominy family in the eighteenth and early nineteenth centuries offer an inight to practices elsewhere.

Kindig, Joseph K., III. *The Philadelphia Chair, 1685-1785*. York, Pennsylvania: The Historical Society of York County, 1978.

Levy, Bernard and S. Dean. *"Opulence and Splendor": The New York Chair, 1690-1830*. New York: Bernard & S. Dean Levy, Inc., 1984.

Miller, V. Isabelle. *Furniture by New York Cabinetmakers: 1650 to 1860*. New York: The Museum of the City of New York, 1956.

Naeve, Milo M. "An Aristocratic Windsor in Eighteenth-Century Philadelphia." *The American Art Journal* 11, no. 3 (July 1979): pages 66-74. Stylistic, technical, and cultural context of a walnut Windsor armchair, currently a unique survival; in this pictorial guide, it is no. 185.

Nakashima, George. *The Soul of a Tree: A Woodworker's Reflections*. Introduction by George Wald. Tokyo: Kodansha International Ltd., 1981. Autobiography of the craftsman who lives in New Hope, Pennsylvania; illustrations of furniture, chronology, awards, exhibitions, selected architectural commissions, bibliography, and glossary.

O'Donnell, Patricia Chapin. "Grisaille decorated *kasten* of New York," *Antiques* CXVII (1980), pages 1108-1111. Six examples dating about 1700 are compared and contrasted; in this pictorial guide, one example is no. 152.

Ostergard, Derek E. *George Nakashima: Full Circle*. Introduction by Sam Maloof; essay by George Nakashima. New York: Weidenfeld & Nicholson, 1989.

Reed, Henry; Yoder, Don; and Fabian, Monroe. *Decorated Furniture of the Mahantongo Valley*. Philadelphia: University of Pennsylvania Press, 1987. Checklist and discussion of all recorded furniture with comment on craftsmen and decorators.

Rice, Norman S. *New York Furniture before 1840 in the Collection of the Albany Institute of History and Art*. Albany: The Albany Institute, 1962.

Scherer, John L. *New York Furniture at the New York State Museum*. Albany: Division of Historical and Anthropological Services, The New York State Museum, The State Education Department, 1984. Furniture dates from 1680-1810, and much of it documented by maker and owner.

————. *New York Furniture: The Federal Period 1788-1825*. Albany: University of the State of New York, 1988. Includes some entries from the author's 1984 publication with many recent accessions.

Schiffer, Margaret Berwind. *Furniture and Its Makers of Chester County, Pennsylvania*. Philadelphia: University of Pennsylvania Press, 1966.

Schwartz, Marvin D.; Stanek, Edward; and True, Douglas. *The Furniture of John Henry Belter and the Rococo Revival*. New York: E. P. Dutton, 1981.

Sewell, Darrel, et al. *Philadelphia: Three Centuries of American Art*. Philadelphia: The Philadelphia Museum of Art, 1976. Furniture entries by Beatrice Garvan, David Hanks, and Page Talbott; the study ranges from 1676 to 1976.

Tracy, Berry B. *Federal Furniture and Decorative Arts at Boscobel*. New York: Boscobel Restoration, Inc., 1981. Furnishings of a restored house near New York City.

Volk, Joyce Geary. "The Dutch Kast and the American Kas: A Structural/Historical Analysis." In *New World Dutch Studies: Dutch Arts and Culture in Colonial America, 1609-1776*, edited by Roderic H. Blackburn and Nancy A. Kelley, pages 107-117. Albany, New York: The Albany Institute of History and Art, 1987.

Wainwright, Nicholas B., with a foreword by Henry Francis du Pont. *Colonial Grandeur in Philadelphia*. Philadelphia: The Historical Society of Pennsylvania, 1964. Documentation for furniture John Cadwalader commissioned 1769-1770 for one of the most lavish American residences of the period.

Waters, Deborah Dependahl, with an introduction by Charles G. Dorman. *Plain and Ornamental: Delaware Furniture 1740-1890*. Wilmington: The Historical Society of Delaware, 1984. Technical notes and illustrations.

White, Margaret E. *Early Furniture Made in New Jersey, 1690-1870*. Newark: The Newark Museum Association, 1958.

Regional Sources: Midwest

Connell, E. Jane, and Muller, Charles R. *Made in Ohio: Furniture, 1788-1888.* Columbus: The Columbus Museum of Art, 1984. Includes bibliography.

Darling, Sharon S. *Chicago Furniture, 1833-1983.* New York: The Chicago Historical Society, in association with W. W. Norton, 1984. Includes bibliography.

Gray, Stephen, editor. *Arts and Crafts Furniture: Shop of the Crafters at Cincinnati.* New York: Turn of the Century Editions, 1983.

Hageman, Jane Sikes. *Ohio Furniture Makers: 1790 to 1845.* Cincinnati, Ohio: Jane Sikes Hageman, 1984.

Miller, R. Craig. "Interior Design and Furniture." In *Design in America: The Cranbrook Vision, 1925-1950,* edited by Adele Westbrook and Anne Yarowsky. New York: Harry N. Abrams, Inc., in association with the Detroit Institute of Arts and the Metropolitan Museum of Art, 1983. Survey of Eliel Saarinen's furniture designs with the founding of the Cranbrook Academy of Art in 1932 and his influence as a teacher, particularly on his son Eero Saarinen, Florence Knoll, and Charles and Ray Eames. The book includes essays on the Cranbrook philosophy, staff, and history with excellent illustrations, documentation, and biographies of the main artists.

Pfeiffer, Bruce Brooks. *The Chairs of Frank Lloyd Wright.* New Haven: Yale University School of Architecture, 1987. Catalogue for an exhibition from November 2-20, 1987. Illustrations include rooms, with other furniture, drawings, and chairs. Introduction includes comments by many individuals concerned with studies about Wright.

Robertson, Cheryl. *The Domestic Scene (1897-1927): George M. Niedecken, Interior Architect.* Milwaukee: The Milwaukee Art Museum, 1981. Study of the life and work of one of Wright's major collaborators; offers a broad insight into the innovative concepts of the Chicago School.

Sikes, Jane E. *The Furniture Makers of Cincinnati, 1790 to 1849.* Cincinnati: Privately printed, 1976.

Spencer, Brian A., editor. *The Prairie School Tradition.* New York: Watson-Guptil Publications, 1979. Emphasis on buildings and related furniture.

Van Ravensway, Charles. *The Arts and Architecture of German Settlements in Missouri: A Survey of a Vanishing Culture.* Columbia: University of Missouri Press, 1979. Furniture discussed in chapter 13, pages 311-393, with the conclusion that colonists made very few objects in peasant traditions, some objects in simplified neoclassical designs, and many objects in vernacular and eclectic styles of the late nineteenth century; includes illustrations and bibliography.

Regional Sources: New England

Churchill, Edwin A. *Simple Forms and Vivid Colors: An Exhibition of Maine Painted Furniture, 1800-1850, at the Maine State Museum, July 8, 1983, through February 28, 1984.* Augusta: The Maine State Museum, 1983.

Clunie, Margaret Burke; Farnam, Anne; and Trent, Robert F. *Furniture at the Essex Institute.* Salem: The Essex Institute, 1980.

Cooke, Edward S., Jr. *Fiddlebacks and Crooked-backs: Elijah Booth and Other Joiners in Newtown and Woodbury, 1750-1820.* Waterbury, Connecticut: The Mattatuck Historical Society, 1982.

Fairbanks, Jonathan L., editor. *New England Begins: The Seventeenth Century.* 3 volumes. Boston: The Museum of Fine Arts, 1982. See Robert Blair St. George, "'Set Thine House in Order': The Domestication of the Yeomanry in Seventeenth-Century New England," volume 2, pages 159-351, and Robert F. Trent, "New England Joinery and Turning before 1700," volume 3, pages 501-550.

Fales, Dean A., Jr. *Essex County Furniture: Documented Treasures from Local Collections, 1660-1860.* Salem: The Essex Institute, 1965.

————. *The Furniture of Historic Deerfield.* New York: E. P. Dutton and Co., 1976. Includes seventeenth, eighteenth, and early nineteenth centuries.

————, et al. *Samuel McIntire: A Bicentennial Symposium, 1757-1957.* Salem: The Essex Institute, 1957.

Garvin, Donna-Belle; Garvin, James L.; and Page, John F. *Plain and Elegant, Rich and Common: Documented New Hampshire Furniture, 1750-1850.* Concord: New Hampshire Historical Society, 1979.

Greenlaw, Barry A. *New England Furniture at Williamsburg.* Williamsburg: The Colonial Williamsburg Foundation, 1974. Includes seventeenth, eighteenth, and early nineteenth centuries.

Jobe, Brock, editor. *New England Furniture: Essays in Memory of Benno M. Forman.* Boston: The Society for the Preservation of New England Antiquities, 1987. Issued as Volume 72 of *Old Time New England.* Essays by Jobe on Portsmouth mid-eighteenth century furniture, Philip Zea on the Hadley chest, Gerald W. R. Ward on Connecticut seventeenth-century furniture, Jeanne Vibert Sloane on Newport furniture, Luke Bekerdite on carving in eighteenth-century Boston, Myrna Kaye on Maine furniture, William N. Hosley, Jr., on Vermont furniture, Robert D. Mussey, Jr., on historic furniture finishes, and Andrew Passeri and Robert F. Trent on upholstery.

_____ , et al. *Elegant Embellishments: Furnishings from New England Homes, 1660-1860.* Boston: The Society for the Preservation of New England Antiquities, 1982.

_____ , and Kaye, Myrna, with the assistance of Philip Zea. *New England Furniture, the Colonial Era: Selections from the Society for the Preservation of New England Antiquities.* Boston: Houghton Mifflin, 1984.

Kane, Patricia E. *Furniture of the New Haven Colony: The Seventeenth-Century Style.* New Haven: The New Haven Colony Historical Society, 1973.

Kenney, John Tarrant. *The Hitchcock Chair.* New York: C. N. Potter, 1971.

Luther, Clair Franklin. *The Hadley Chest.* Hartford: Privately printed, 1935. For recent research, see above, Patricia E. Kane in Quimby, *Arts of the Anglo-American Community in the Seventeenth Century;* Richard Lawrence Green, "Fertility Symbols on the Hadley Chests," *Antiques,* 112 (August 1977): pages 250-257; and Philip Zea in Jobe, *New England Furniture.*

Maynard, Henry P., and Kirk, John T. *Connecticut Furniture: Seventeenth and Eighteenth Centuries.* Hartford: Wadsworth Atheneum, 1967.

Moses, Michael. *Master Craftsmen of Newport: The Townsends and Goddards.* Tenafly, New Jersey: Michael Moses Americana Press and Israel Sack, Inc., 1984.

Ott, Joseph K., et al. *The John Brown House Loan Exhibition of Rhode Island Furniture.* Providence: The Rhode Island Historical Society, 1965.

Parsons, Charles S. *The Dunlaps and Their Furniture.* Manchester, New Hampshire: The Currier Gallery of Art, 1970.

St. George, Robert Blair. *The Wrought Covenant: Source Material for the Study of Craftsmen and Community in Southeastern New England, 1620-1700.* Brockton, Massachusetts: The Brockton Art Center and Fuller Memorial, 1979.

Sander, Penny J., editor. *Elegant Embellishments: Furnishings from New England Homes, 1660-1860.* Boston: The Society for the Preservation of New England Antiquities, 1982. Selections from Society collections. For more recent information about colonial furniture, see Brock Jobe, et al., *New England Furniture, the Colonial Era,* but the publication is the only compilation of the significant post-colonial furniture owned by the society.

Trent, Robert F. *Folk Chairs of the Connecticut Coast, 1720-1840, as Viewed in the Light of Henry Focillon's Introduction to* Art Populaire. New Haven: The New Haven Colony Historical Society, 1977.

_____ . "The Endicott Chairs." In *Essex Institute Historical Collections,* 114, no. 2 (April 1978): pages 103-119. Documentation for the armchair published as no. 16 in this pictorial guide, with information about production of other chairs in Boston from 1660 to 1695.

_____ , and Nelson, Nancy Lee. *New London County Joined Chairs, 1720-1790.* Hartford, Connecticut: The Connecticut Historical Society and the Lyman Allyn Museum, 1985. Catalogue for an exhibition at The Connecticut Historical Society October 1-December 24, 1985, and the Lyman Allyn Museum January 15-February 28, 1986, issued as volume 50, no. 4 (Fall 1985) of *The Connecticut Historical Society Bulletin.*

Whitehill, Walter Muir, editor, assisted by Brock Jobe. *Boston Furniture of the Eighteenth Century.* Boston: The Colonial Society of Massachusetts, 1974. Written by nine specialists, the book presents research resulting from a conference and exhibition organized by Jonathan L. Fairbanks on the organization of furniture industry, forms, decoration, and woods; includes a checklist of craftsmen and a bibliography for individual craftsmen.

Zea, Philip. "Furniture." In *The Great River: Art & Society of the Connecticut Valley, 1635-1820.* Hartford: Wadsworth Atheneum, 1985.

Regional Sources: South

Albright, Frank P. *Johann Ludwig Eberhardt and His Salem Clocks.* Winston-Salem, North Carolina: Old Salem, Inc., 1978.

Atlanta Historical Society. *Neat Pieces: The Plain-Style Furniture of 19th Century Georgia.* Atlanta: The Atlanta Historical Society, 1983.

[Bacot, H. Parrott.] *Southern Furniture and Silver: The Federal Period, 1788-1830.* Baton Rouge, Louisiana: The Anglo-American Art Museum of Louisiana State University, 1968.

Baltimore Museum of Art. *Baltimore Furniture: The Work of Baltimore and Annapolis Cabinetmakers from 1760 to 1810.* Baltimore: The Baltimore Museum of Art, 1947.

Bivins, John. *Furniture of Coastal North Carolina, 1700-1820.* Winston-Salem, North Carolina: The Museum of Early Southern Decorative Arts, 1988.

Burton, E. Milby. *Charleston Furniture, 1700-1825.* Charleston, South Carolina: The Charleston Museum, 1955.

Coons, Betty C. *Antique By-Lines (Southern Vintage).* Richmond: The Guild of the Valentine Museum, 1979.

Elder, William Voss, III. *Baltimore Painted Furniture, 1800-1840.* Baltimore, Maryland: The Baltimore Museum of Art, 1972.

_____ , and Bartlett, Lu. *John Shaw: Cabinetmaker of Annapolis.* Baltimore, Maryland: The Baltimore Museum of Art, 1983. Excellent study of the foremost craftsman (1745-1829) in the capital; sixty-one objects traced to the shop.

_____ . *Maryland Queen Anne and Chippendale Furniture of the Eighteenth Century.* Baltimore, Maryland: October House, Inc., for the Baltimore Museum of Art, 1968.

_____ ; Stokes, Jayne E.; et al. *American Furniture 1680-1800: From the Collection of the Baltimore Museum of Art.* Baltimore, Maryland: The Baltimore Museum of Art, 1986. Technical notes, essays, and illustrations of over-all views, details, and related objects elsewhere.

Fitzgerald, Oscar P. *Greene Family of Cabinetmakers: An Alexandria Institution 1817-1887.* Alexandria, Virginia: Alexandria Association, 1986.

Green, Henry D. *Furniture of the Georgia Piedmont Before 1830.* Atlanta: The High Museum of Art, 1976.

Gusler, Wallace B. *Furniture of Williamsburg and Eastern Virginia, 1710-1790.* Richmond: The Virginia Museum, 1979.

Horton, Frank L. *The Museum of Early Southern Decorative Arts.* Winston-Salem, North Carolina: The Museum of Early Southern Decorative Arts, 1979. Furniture included in room views, as the subject of illustrations, and in commentaries.

Lohr, N. Gordon; Melchor, James R.; and Melchor, Marilyn S. *Eastern Shore, Virginia, Raised-Panel Furniture, 1730-1830.* Norfolk: The Chrysler Museum, 1982.

North Carolina Museum of History. *North Carolina Furniture.* Raleigh: The North Carolina Museum of History, 1977.

Page, Addison Franklin. *Kentucky Furniture.* Louisville: The J. B. Speed Art Museum, 1974.

Piorkowski, Patricia Ann. *Piedmont Virginia Furniture: Product of Provincial Cabinetmakers.* Lynchburg, Virginia: Lynchburg Museum System, 1982.

Poesch, Jessie J. *The Art of the Old South: Painting, Sculpture, Architecture & the Products of Craftsmen, 1560-1860.* New York: Alfred A. Knopf, 1983. Documented and illustrated survey, with excellent bibliography, that includes furniture.

_____ . *Early Furniture of Louisiana, 1750-1830.* New Orleans: The Louisiana State Museum, 1972.

Theus, Mrs. Charlton M. *Savannah Furniture, 1735-1825.* Savannah, Georgia: Privately printed, 1967.

Weidman, Gregory R. *Furniture in Maryland, 1740-1940: The Collection of the Maryland Historical Society.* Baltimore: The Maryland Historical Society, 1984. Technical notes, essays, and illustrations; emphasis on furniture made in Maryland but includes furniture made elsewhere.

Williams, Derita Coleman and Harsh, Nathan. *The Art and Mystery of Tennessee Furniture and Its Makers Through 1850.* Nashville: The Tennessee Historical Society and the Tennessee State Museum Foundation, 1988. Includes color illustrations and a checklist of craftsmen through 1850.

Winters, Robert E., editor. *North Carolina Furniture, 1700-1900.* Raleigh: The North Carolina Museum of History, Division of Archives and History, Department of Cultural Resources, 1977.

Regional Sources: Southwest

Steinfeldt, Cecilia, and Stover, Donald. *Early Texas Furniture and Decorative Arts.* San Antonio: The San Antonio Museum Association, [1973].

Taylor, Lonn, and Bokides, Dessa, with an introduction by Jonathan L. Fairbanks. *New Mexican Furniture, 1600-1940: The Origins, Survival, and Revival of Furniture Making in the Hispanic Southwest.* Santa Fe: Museum of New Mexico Press, 1987. Authoritative, documented survey with excellent illustrations, many in color.

_____ , and Warren, David B. *Texas Furniture: The Cabinetmakers and Their Work, 1840-1880.* Austin: University of Texas Press, 1975. Thorough bibliography.

Vedder, Alan C. *Furniture of Spanish New Mexico.* Santa Fe: Sunstone Press, 1977. For information about the background and types, see Taylor and Bokides; however, this book includes privately owned furniture not illustrated elsewhere.

Regional Sources: West

Anderson, Timothy J., et al. *California Design, 1910.* Los Angeles: California Design Center, 1974.

Jones, Harvey L. *California Woodworking: An Exhibition of Contemporary Handcrafted Furniture.* Oakland: The Oakland Museum, 1980.

Makinson, Randell L. *Greene & Greene: Furniture and Related Designs.* Volume 2. Salt Lake City: Gibbs M. Smith, Inc., Peregrine Smith Books, 1979.

Maloof, Sam. *Sam Maloof: Woodworker.* Introduction by Jonathan L. Fairbanks. Tokyo: Kodansha International Ltd., 1983. Autobiography with illustrations of furniture and procedures.

Morningstar, Connie. *Early Utah Furniture.* Logan: Utah State University Press, 1976.

Bold face references are to page numbers; others are to illustrations. Craftsmen, designers and manufacturers are included. Forms are selectively represented. Motifs are cited by major interpretations in differing periods. Styles are easily located through the table of contents, and the reader is advised to consult commentaries pertinent to an inquiry.

Acanthus
   leaf, 31, 51, 70; **5**
   scroll, 87, **13**
Acorn motif, 179
Adirondack furniture type, 177; **65**
Alacena, **61**
Aluminum, 137
Amboina veneer, 85
Anodized steel, 144
Anthemion, 51, 90, 91, 92, 94
Antique French Style, **27**
Apron (skirt), 11, 23, 28, 33, 74, 173
Arch
   Gothic, 51, 59, 61, 62, 63, 64
   lancet, 51, 63, 194
   ogee, 62, 64
   Roman, 9, 18, 62, 100
   trefoil, 61, 62
Armchair, 1, 3, 7, 16, 19, 47, 61, 68, 69, 81, 86, 92, 95, 101, 106, 115, 123, 128, 130, 131, 132, 137, 151, 161, 164, 169, 177, 184, 185
Arts and Crafts Movement, **45, 47, 53**
Astragal
   bead, 11, 13, 52
   double bead, 18

Babson House, Henry B., 104

Ball-and-ring turning, 17
Ball foot, 9, 11, 12, 13, 15, 18, 21, 88, 99, 106, 123, 128, 150, 152, 155, 168
Ball turning, 16, 69
Baluster turning, 2, 3, 19, 22, 65, 88, 184
   double baluster, 22, 168
   whorled, 45
Bamboo turning, 108, 186
Banding, 21, 24, 125
   machine, 59
Baroque, **viii, 7, 9, 27**
Basket-of-flowers motif, 74, 76, 78
Batten, 157, 158, 165, 166
Baudouine, Charles A. (cabinetmaker), 87
Bauhaus, the, **51**
Bead (astragal) molding, 11, 13, 52
   double, 18
Bedstead
   lowpost, 175, 179; **5, 65**
   highpost, 27; **5**
   other, 48, 79, 93, 108
   survival, **xi, 3**
Belter, John Henry (cabinetmaker), 76, 77, 78, 79
Bertoia, Harry (designer), 132
Bevel, 15
Bing, Siegfried, and Art Nouveau Style, 43
Birch veneer, 40
Blacker House, Robert R., 119
Blind fret, 176
Block, Leigh B. (apartment), 127
Block front design, 24, 30, 34
Bombé case form, 35
Bookcase, 102, 103
Boss, 9, 15, 92, 94, 150
Box, 6; **3, 5**
Brace, on Windsor chair back, 184

Bracket, 28, 31, 102, 103, 119
Bracket foot
   ogee, 30, 32, 34, 157, 158
   straight, 24, 158, 180
Brass
   band, 45
   inlay, 104
   tacks (upholstery), 16, 19
Breakfast table, 114
Breuer, Marcel (architect and designer), **51**
Brigden, Robert, and design book, **25**
Broken-arch pediment, 24, 26, 32, 33, 157, 173, 176
Bronze head, 95, 98
Brooks, Thomas (cabinetmaker), 64
Bryent, Walter (designer), 75
Bureau table, 34
Butterfly table, 168
Byrne, Richard (cabinetmaker), 60

C Scroll, 19, 29, 31, 71, 73, 79; **9, 13, 27, 29**
Cabinet, 83, 84, 94, 110
Cabriole leg, 25, 29, 54, 70, 78, 87, 113, 167, 171, 172, 174, 181, 185, 191
Caming, 121
Caning, 46
Canted corners, 45, 50, 58
Cantilever (seat), 123
Card table, 29, 41, 42, 49, 55, 82; **11, 13, 15**
Cartouche, 71, 73
Castle, Wendell, 138, 143, 145; **55**
Castor, 39, 53, 55, 64, 69, 74, 80, 81, 85, 86, 92, 95
Cavetta molding, 22
Center table, 11, 74, 75, 76, 78, 98
Ceramic decoration, 83, 84, 103
Chair-Table, 153; **5, 57**

Chamber table, 12
Chamfer, 2, 25, 33, 99, 101, 102, 154
Channel molding, 11, 161
Chapin, Aaron and Eliphalet
    (cabinetmakers), 172
Chase Brothers and Co. (foundry), 75
Chest, 4, 10, 158, 159, 160, 163, 165
    six-board, **3**
    slab-end, **3**
    table, 142, 153
Chest of drawers, 12, 15, 35, 44, 62, 66,
    107, 142
Chest-on-chest, 167
Chicago Arts and Crafts Society, 121
Child, furniture for,
    high chair, 5, 170
    Windsor side chair, 188
Chip carving, 6; **3**
Chippendale, Thomas (cabinetmaker), **13**
Chrome, 128, 133
Clark, Edward Ellefson (designer), 147; **55**
Clark, John, (piano maker), 89
Claw-and-ball foot, 29, 31, 33, 35, 68, 95,
    172, 176; **11, 13**
Cleat, 4, 10, 12, 156
Clock, 32, 104, 173
Cloven-hoof foot, 90
Cluster column, 62, 89, 97
Cocktail table, 127
Coffee table, 133, 136
Collarino, 8, 23
Color, in furniture, **5, 7, 11, 25, 55, 57, 59,**
    61, 63, 65, 69
Colt Willow Ware Works, 194
Column
    cluster, 62, 89
    Doric, 8, 32, 184

Ionic, 85
    octagonal, 59
    quarter-, 32
    Tuscan, 19
Columnar footposts, 27
Company of Master Craftsmen, 129
Compass
    inlay, 21
    seat shape, 25
Concentric circle motif, 57, 58
Connecticut River Valley, **63**
Conner, Robert, and design book, **23**
Console motif, 73, 88
Coonley House, Avery, 125
Corner chair, 113
Cornice, 18, 32, 40, 51, 100, 107, 152, 155,
    167
Cornucopia, 46, 53
Cottage furniture, **25**
Couch, 53; **11, 13**
Cradle-cabinet, 141
Crest (chair), 19
Crest rail, 25, 31, 54, 171, 185
Crocket, 60, 100, 112
Croome, George (cabinetmaker), 94
Cross stretchers, 154
Cupboard, 9, 162
Curule chair, 92
Cyma
    curve, 169
    recta molding, 22
    reversa molding, 20

Davis, Alexander Jackson (architect and
    designer), 60
Daybed *(méridienne)*, 57
Demi-Lune (table), 138

Dennis, Thomas (joiner), 7
Dentil, 155
Desk, 21, 30, 116, 125, 180
Desk and bookcase, 18, 24, 40, 51, 157, 176;
    9
Deskey, Donald (designer), 126, 128
Dessoir, Julius (cabinetmaker), 88
Dial (clock), 32, 104, 173
Dining chair, 183
Dining table, 2, 22, 59, 129; **9, 11**
    extension, 59
Disc, on turned pad foot, 28
Doe, Hazelton and Co. (cabinetmakers), 74
Dog foot, 44
Dolphin motif, 48
Doric column, 8, 32, 184
Double baluster turning, 22, 168
Dovetail joint, 163
Dressing table, 28
Drop, 20, 26, 61
Dunlap, Samuel (cabinetmaker), 167

Eagle motif, 53
Eames, Charles (designer), 135; **51**
Eastlake, Charles Locke, and publications
    about taste, **39**
Easy chair, 17, 144
Easy Chair (title), 144
Egg-and-dart motif, 6, 83, 176
Egyptian stool form, 96
Elliptic front, 44
    triple, 42
Ellis, Harvey (designer), 120
Elmslie, George Grant (architect and
    designer), 104, 123, 124
Emery Shops (woodworkers), 9
Enfield, Connecticut, Shaker Colony, 181

England, influence on furniture design, x
Esherick, Wharton (designer), 140, 142; **53**
Étagère, 63, 70, 73, 88
Evans Products Co. (furniture manufacturer), 135
Extension table, 59

Face (clock), 32, 104, 173
Feick, George (architect), 123
Festoon (swag), 26, 36, 159, 176
Fielded panel, 18, 100, 107, 150, 160
Finial
    bed, 93, 109, 179
    bookcase, 103
    chair, 5, 7, 18, 19, 61, 151, 169
    chest of drawers, 62
    clock, 32, 104
    desk and bookcase, 24, 40, 157, 176
    étagère, 63, 73, 88
    high chest of drawers, 26, 33
    settee, 64
    sideboard, 100
    urn-shaped, 18, 24, 26
Fire screen, **13**
Flint, George C., and Co., 110
Flitch (veneer), 20, 21
Floral motif, 33, 70, 74, 76, 77, 82, 89, 100, 105, 109, 110, 113, 118, 159, 165, 166; **5, 13, 15, 23, 27, 29, 31, 43, 63**
Fluting, 31, 32, 33, 37, 65, 82, 107, 158
Flying buttress, 103
Foliate scroll, 7, 158, 163
Footboard (bed), 79, 179
Footrest, 170
France, influence on furniture design, **x, 19, 21, 27, 31, 33, 35, 43, 49**
Fret (Chinese), 172, 176

Fruit motif, 74

Gadrooning, 29, 51
Gaming table, 29
Garden table, 192
Gate-leg table, 22; **9, 11, 13**
Germany, influence on furniture design, **x, 27, 29, 49, 51, 19**
Godwin, E. W., and Art Furniture, **41, 45**
Gore, Gary (editor), **ix**
Gothic (pointed) arch, 51, 59, 61, 62, 63, 64
Gothic Style garden furniture, 190; **71**
Gould, Royal H. (cabinetmaker), 41
Grand Rapids Chair Co., 130
Grapes-and-leaves motif, 77, 78, 80
Great chair, 1, 3, 7, 169
Grecian lounge, 53
Greek curule shape, 90, 92
Greek key motif, 94
Greene, Charles Sumner (architect and designer), 117, 119
Grooves, 102
Gropius, Walter (architect), **51**
Grotesque, 7, 87

Hadley chest, 166; **63**
Hagen, Ernest and J. Matthew Meier (workshop), 114, 115
Haircloth upholstery, 53
Hall, John, and design book, **21**
Hall, Peter and John (cabinetmakers), 117
Handgrip, 156
Hazelton (Doe, Hazelton and Co., cabinetmaker), 74
Headboard (bed), 27, 79, 175, 179
Heart motif, **59, 63**
Herman Miller Furniture Co., 133, 136

Herringbone banding, 21, 125
Herter Brothers (cabinetmakers and decorators), 65, 100, 105, 109
Hickory (bark), 178
High chair, 5, 170
High chest of drawers, 13, 20, 26, 33
Hitchcock chair factory, **65**
Hoadley, Silas (clockmaker), 173
Homes, William and Co. (cabinetmakers), 102
Hoof foot, 90; **33**
Hound-chasing-fox motif, 74
Hudson River Valley, **57**
Hull House (Chicago), 121
Husk, 37, 39

Ice cream, 148; **55**
Indian stepped design, 164
Inlay, 21, 24, 37, 39, 40, 41, 49, 65, 85, 117, 119, 129, 155, 158, 176; **9, 15, 19, 35, 41, 45**
Ionic column, 85
Iron, furniture made of, 75, 190, 191, 192, 193, 196; **27, 71**
Italy, influence on furniture design, **5, 55**
Ivory, **31**

Jackson, Daniel K. (cabinetmaker), 139
Jacques, Stephen (joiner), 8
Japan, influence on furniture design, **41, 43**
Japanese laquer, 109
Japanning, 26; **9, 11, 13**
Jelliff, John (cabinetmaker), 86
Johnson, Thomas (Japanner), 26
Joint stool, 8

Kas (wardrobe), 150, 152; **57**

Klismos (chair), 52; **19, 21**
Knoll, Hammond (designer), 131
Knoll International, 132, 137
Knurling, 38
Kramer, Helen Knoll, 131
Kramer Brothers (foundry), 196

Laminated woods, 70, 77, 78, 79, 80, 87, 134, 135, 141, 143, 146; **xi**
Lancet arch, 51, 63, 194
Lannuier, Charles-Honoré (cabinetmaker), 48, 49
Larkin Building (Buffalo, New York), furniture for, 122
Leaf design, 10, 19, 31, 33, 42, 43, 46, 166, 171
Leather
  surface, 127
  upholstery, 16, 19, 56, 115, 122, 123, 130
Le Grand Lockwood House, 65
Lewis, James Angivine (designer), 147; **55**
Lewis & Clark (designers), 147; **55**
Library chair, 56
Library table, 76, 85, 118
Liebes, Dorothy (textile designer and weaver), 128
Linden Glass Co., 121
Linenfold carving, 118
Lion motif, 42, 43, 45, 46, 49, 92, 98, 109, 163
Livery cupboards, 3
Long Island, **57**
Looking glass, 139
Loper, 18, 21, 24, 30, 40, 157
Lotus motif, 97
Louis Quatorze Style, **27**
Louis Quinze Style, **27**

Lozenge, 9, 31
Lucky Table (title), 145
Lunette, 10
Lyre-shaped splat, 43

Machine
  banding, 59
  and furniture, **x-xi**, 39, 45, 47, 51, 53, 55, **65**
McIntire, Samuel (carver), 36
Maher, George Washington (architect), 118
Maison de l'Art Nouveau, **43**
Maloof, Sam (cabinetmaker), 141
Marcotte, Leon (cabinetmaker), 81, 83, 85
Marlborough foot, **13**
Marot, Daniel (designer), **9**
Marquand, Henry G., 107
Marquetry, 84, 105, 109
Marx, Samuel (designer), 127
  apartment, 128
Mask
  female head, 86
  grotesque, 87
Mathews, Lucia K., and Arthur F. (designers), 116
Medial stretcher, 17, 19, 25, 68, 85, 92, 93, 98, 112, 119, 130, 134, 153, 171, 184
Meeks, John and Joseph W. (firm of), 80
Meier, J. Matthew and Ernest Hagen (workshop), 114, 115
Memphis (designers), **55**
Merchant's Bank (Winona, Minnesota), 123
Méridienne (daybed), 57
Mésangère, Pierre de la, and design periodical, **21**
Mexico City, **61**
Miller, Herman, Co. (furniture

manufacturers), 133, 136
Mirror, 58, 62, 63, 66, 70, 71, 73, 88, 139
Modern Greek Style, **35**
Molding
  applied, 23
  astragal (bead), 11, 13, 25, 52
  astragal (double bead), 8, 18, 21
  cavetta, 20
  channel, 11, 161
  cyma, 22
  cyma recta, 125
  cyma reversa, 20, 26, 28
  ogee, 125, 167
  ovolo, 13
  scotia, **5**
  torus, **5**
Morris, William, **39, 45**
Mortise-and-tenon joint, 10, 162
Moser, Koloman (designer), **47**
Mount Lebanon Shaker Colony, 179, 182, 183; **67**
Mullion, 10
Muntin, 40, 51, 176
Museum of Modern Art, design competition of, **51**
Music cabinet, 94
Music rack, 140
Myers, Forrest (designer and sculptor), 144

Nakashima, George (cabinetmaker), 189
Near East, influence on furniture design, 41
Needlework upholstery, 67
Nelson, George (designer), 133
Nelson, Matter, and Co. (furniture manufacturers), 93
Neopolitan Table (title), 148
Netherlands, the, 57

New Greek Style, **35**
Niedecken, George M. (designer), 121, 125; **41, 45, 47**
Noguchi, Isamu (designer), 136
Nordness, Lee (apartment), 143
Norman (style), **23**
Nunns, Robert (piano maker), 89

Oak-leaves-and-acorn motif, 77, 79
Ogee arch, 62, 64
Ogee molding, 125, 167
Orb, winged, 98
Ormolu, 48, 49, 50, 51, 56, 81, 83, 84, 85
Ovolo molding, 13, 150, 176
Owner
    initials, 12, 159
    name and date, 155

Pad foot, 25, 27, 28, 185
    square, 167
Paintbrush foot, 17, 22
Palmette, 52
Panel (mirrored glass), 24, 110
Patera, 37, 159
Paw foot (lion), 26, 42, 43, 45, 46, 49, 98, 109
Payne, Lee (designer), 148; **55**
Pedestal, 91, 99; **21**
    card table support, 55
    chair support, 137
Pediment
    broken arch, 24, 26, 33, 173, 176
    double arch, 18
    with hood, 18
Pembroke table, 39
Pendant, 20, 23, 26, 61, 112
Perkins, Larry (designer), 134

Phidias Chair (title), 149
Phyfe, Duncan (cabinetmaker)
    furniture by, 45, 47, 57, 58
    style of, **16-17**
Piano, 50, 89
Pier
    mirror, 71
    table, 58
Pilaster, 24, 40, 92, 158
Pimm, John (cabinetmaker), 26
Plastic, 137, 146, 147, 148
Plinth, 62, 94
Pomegranate motif, 165
Pop Art, 148; **55**
Poppy motif, 110
Portuguese foot, 17, 22
Press cupboard, 9
Price books (London: 1802; 1808), **17**
Pugin, A. W., and design book, **23**
Purcell, William Gray (designer), 104, 123
Putti, 77, 107

Quatrefoil, 61, 64
Quervelle, Antoine Gabriel (cabinetmaker), 51
Quigley, William (company), 127

Rabbit motif, 167
Radio City Music Hall, 126
Rail
    chair (front, side, crest), 25, 31, 171, 172, 184
    chest, 10, 166
Recessed seat (cushion), 14
Reeding, 38, 44, 45, 46, 47, 53, 106
Reel turning, 12
Regional characteristics, **11, 13, 19**

Relief carving, 7, 9, 118, 166
Repiso, **61**
Robert R. Blacker House, 119
Robert Wood and Co. (foundry), 191
Rocking chair, 120, 178, 182, 187
Rococo Style
    carving, 29, 31, 32, 33; **13, 27**
    garden furniture, 191; **71**
    motifs, **13, 25, 27, 43, 45**
Rohlfs, Charles (designer), 112
Roman arch, 9, 62, 100
Rope, 175
Rose, flowers and leaves as motifs, 70, 77, 109
Rosette, 33, 47, 52, 165
Roux, Alexander (cabinetmaker), 82, 84, 90
Rudolph, Emil (house), 118
Rush seat, 151, 169, 170, 183
Rustic furniture, 177, 178; **65**

S Scroll, 71, 73, 79, 167; **13, 27, 29**
Saarinen, Eero (architect and designer), 134, 137; **51**
Saarinen, Eliel (architect and designer), 129
Saltire stretcher, 74, 75, 78, 194
Satinwood veneer, 38, 48
Savery, William (cabinetmaker), 171
Scallop shell, 26, 28, 30, 31, 33, 34, 73, 74, 75, 167, 172
Scott, Isaac E. (cabinetmaker), 103
Scott, Sir Walter, **25**
Scrolled pediment (broken arch), 24, 26, 32, 33, 157, 173, 176
Scroll foot, 55, 72, 87, 192, 195
Scrutoir (desk), 21
Serpentine curve, 35, 37, 73, 77, 79, 176
Serving table, 117

Settee, 46, 64, 186, 190, 194, 196
Settle, 3
Shaw, Henry, and furniture book, **25**
Shearer, John (cabinetmaker), 176
Shell. *See* Scallop shell.
Shield-shaped chair back, 36
Shire, Peter (designer), 149; **55**
Shoe (chair back), 25, 31
Shonk (wardrobe), 155; **59**
Shoulder (chair), 25
Sideboard, 37, 100, 109
Side chair, 25, 31, 36, 43, 52, 54, 60, 65, 67,
    72, 77, 105, 112, 119, 122, 124, 134,
    135, 146, 156, 171, 172, 188, 189, 191,
    195
Silk damask upholstery, 72, 77, 81, 87, 105
Skirt (apron), 11, 23, 28, 33, 74, 87, 173
Slat-back chairs, 151, 169, 182, 183
Slide
    for candlestick, 18, 24
    for work surface, 180
Slipper foot, 23
Slip seat, 25, 31, 43, 52, 113, 119
Smith, George, and design book, **21**
Sofa, 80, 87, 143; **11, 15, 21**
Spade foot, 36
Spandrel (clock), 32, 104, 173
Spanish foot, 17, 22
Sphinx motif, 49
Spindle, 1, 3, 5, 13, 14, 100, 108, 162, 164;
    3, 39, 61, 69
    split, 12, 66; **5**
Spiral turning, 13, 14, 67, 68
Splat, 25, 31, 43, 54, 119, 161, 171, 172
Splay leg, 168
Splint seat, 1, 3, 182
Split spindle, 9, 12, 66; **5**
Spooner, Sherlock, and George Trask

(cabinetmakers), 52
Stands, 91, 111, 181
Star inlay, 21
Steel, 144
Stencil decoration, 187; **65**
Stewart, James (piano maker), 50
Stickley, Gustav (furniture manufacturer),
    120
Stile
    chair, 19, 25, 31
    chest, 10, 166
Stipple background, 10, 107
Stool, 8, 90, 96, 97; **3**
Strapwork, 7, 65, 67, 89
Stretcher (side, front, medial), 1, 2, 14, 17,
    19, 20, 25, 68, 85, 91, 92, 98, 112, 119,
    130, 134, 153, 168, 171, 184. *See also*
    Saltire stretcher.
Stringing, 39, 41
Suez Canal, **37**
Sulphur inlay, 158; **59**
Swags, 36, 46, 159

Table
    breakfast, 114
    bureau, 34
    "butterfly", 168; **63**
    card, 29, 41, 42, 49, 55, 82; **11, 13, 15**
    center, 11, 74, 75, 76, 78, 98
    chair-table, 153; **5, 57**
    chamber, 12
    cocktail, 127
    coffee, 133, 148
    dining, 2, 22, 59, 129; **9, 11, 15**
    draw, **5**
    dressing, 28
    Dutch Style, 154; **57**
    extension, 59

gaming, 29
garden, 192
gate leg, 22; **9, 11, 13**
library, 76, 85, 118
pedestal, 55; **21**
Pembroke, **15**
pier, 58
serving, 117
Spanish Style, **61**
tea, 23; **9, 11**
trestle, 2; **3, 67**
Windsor, **69**
work, 38
Taos, Ranchos de (church), 160
Tapestry upholstery, 95
Tarmitas, **61**
Tassel motif, 86
Tea table, 23; **9, 11**
Technology, **x-xi**
Tester (bed), 27
Tiffany, Louis Comfort (designer), 114, 115
    apartment, 114, 115
    studios, 106
Townsend, John (cabinetmaker), 34
Trask, George, and Sherlock Spooner
    (cabinetmakers), 52
Trasteros, **61**
Trefoil arch, 61, 62
Trestle base, 2, 153, 189; **9, 11**
Triangle motif, 95, 98, 102, 124, 160
Trifid foot, 171
Triple elliptic front, 42
Tulip motif, 118, 159, 166

Urn, 18, 19, 24, 26, 36, 39, 42, 54, 85, 89,
    171, 193

Valdez, Franciso A. (woodworker), 160

van der Rohe, Miës (architect and designer), **51**

Van Dorn Iron Works, 193

Velvet
  cushion, 16
  upholstery, 17

Veneer, 20, 21, 37, 38, 40, 48, 50, 51, 57, 62, 85

Venturi, Robert (designer and architect), 146; **55**

Vernacular styles, defined, **x**

Volute, 19, 31, 184

W. P. A. Craft Project (Illinois), 134

Walbridge, John S. (decorator), 104, 125; **45, 47**

Wardrobe, 150, 152, 155; **57, 59**

Water leaf, 42, 43, 46

Wave pattern (classical), 30

Weber, Kem (designer), 130

Wheel shape motif, 60

Whiplash curve, 111, 112, 113

Willow, as furniture material, 194

Windsor tables, **69**

Wood, Robert (foundry), 191

Wooden pins, 10

Work table, 38

Wright, Ambrose (cabinetmaker), 60

Wright, Frank Lloyd (architect and designer), 121, 122; **47**
  lecture by, 121

Writing stand,174

Yoke (chair), 25, 171

Zanetti, John (cabinetmaker), 138

Zoar, Ohio (as German colony), 156